Dual-Language Learners

Strategies for Teaching English

Angèle Sancho Passe

Redleaf Press®
www.redleafpress.org
800-423-8309

Published by Redleaf Press
10 Yorkton Court
St. Paul, MN 55117
www.redleafpress.org

First edition 2013
Cover design by Jim Handrigan
Cover photograph © Corbis Photography/Veer
Interior design by Douglas Schmitz
Typeset in ITC Mendoza
Printed in the United States of America
19 18 17 16 15 14 13 12   1 2 3 4 5 6 7 8

Library of Congress Cataloging-in-Publication Data
Passe, Angèle Sancho.
    Dual-language learners : strategies for teaching English / Angèle Sancho Passe. —
1st ed.
        p. cm.
    Includes bibliographical references.
    ISBN 978-1-60554-101-3 (alk. paper)
    1. English language—Study and teaching—Foreign speakers. 2. Education, Bilingual.
    3. Bilingualism in children.   I. Title.
    PE1128.A2P327 2012
    428.0071—dc23
                                                2012025628

Printed on acid-free paper

To Matthew and Alexander,
and all children learning two languages at home and at school

Contents

Acknowledgments

Writing and publishing a book is the ultimate group effort, and many people play a part in the process.

First, I want to thank the leaders at Redleaf Press for their interest in and commitment to this project: Linda Hein, David Heath, and Kyra Ostendorf. I am immensely grateful for my editors: Laurie Herrmann for her precise questions and her steady support, Christine Zuchora-Walske for her confident pen, and Carla Valadez for the final touches

I have worked with many colleagues who have shared my passion for teaching dual-language learners and supporting their families. These colleagues have all contributed with their questions, ideas, challenges, and wisdom. I especially thank Julie Anderson, Anita Beaton, Jackie Blahnick, Julie Buresh, Victoria Campoverde, Camila Carrasco, Catherine Cuddeback, Nery Donis, Becky Drong, Lisa Gruenewald, Marian Hassan, Kate Horst, Laura Johansson, Katie Knutson, Mary Mackedanz, Andi Matre, Kathleen O'Donnell, Gaby Ortega, Annie Pearson, Susan Rydell, Beth Sandell, Maureen Seiwert, Sandy Simar, Beth Standford, Patricia Torres Ray, Yer Vang, Carol Will, and Cory Woosley.

Finally, a big thank-you to my multilingual family, who nurture me with grace and wit, always with the right words. *Merci, gracias,* thank you!

Introduction

In my family, everyone is multilingual. Economic need, personal interest, and political misfortune have inspired my family members to learn French, Arabic, Spanish, German, English, and Catalan over the past four generations.

My life experiences have shaped my language acquisition and multicultural thinking. I was born in French Algeria. My family became refugees in Spain during the Algerian War (1954–62), when I was a child. I immigrated to the United States as an adult. My first language is French. My second is Spanish. My third is English. My adult children are bilingual in French and English. My Minnesotan grandchildren are, too.

I started my teaching career as a French and Spanish instructor. Later I worked as an early childhood teacher, parent educator, and administrator in programs serving both U.S.-born and immigrant families. I have also taught college courses and written publications on dual-language learning. As an education consultant, I meet with and survey immigrant families and educators, and I observe, film, and assess classrooms and child care homes. My specialty is the multilingual classroom in which the children are learning English together but speak different languages at home. I cherish watching children learn, and I enjoy training and coaching their teachers. Helping monolingual and bilingual teachers understand their role, discover their strengths, and use their skills effectively is always rewarding.

Why I Wrote This Book

In this book, I share with you both research evidence and personal insights. I propose a thoughtful, commonsense approach to help young children learn English, maintain their home language, and develop the early literacy skills necessary for school readiness and success.

Teaching language to help young children become bilingual and bi-literate is a challenging task. Educators must bridge school literacy and home language while encouraging parents to use their home language. They must use concrete techniques designed for teaching dual-language learners and supporting their families. Intentionality is critical. A hopeful but haphazard approach often frustrates and disappoints students and families as well as educators.

When I present workshops for educators, I ask them to tell me why they have come. Their responses boil down to two basic questions:

1. What are the best ways to teach children who are dual-language learners?

2. What are the best ways to communicate with and support the families of dual-language learners?

> **The Term *Dual-Language Learner***
>
> I use the term *dual-language learner* rather than the familiar terms *English-language learner* (ELL) or *limited English proficiency* (LEP). I believe *dual-language learner* is the right word to describe a child who is learning both English and a home language. It respects the importance of both languages. English is the practical language needed to succeed in school and the wider world. The home language is the emotional language needed for maintaining family relationships, values, and traditions.

I hope to answer these key questions in this book. As you read, you will probably confirm things you already know. You will also learn some new ideas. I hope you will reflect on your current work and decide how to connect what you know with what you do. Together, you and I can improve the education of young children who are dual-language learners!

Focus and Philosophy

In this book, I address educators in multilingual early childhood classrooms who teach in English and support home languages intentionally. I take into account the challenge of supporting home languages without staff who speak these languages or media produced in them. I describe simple techniques you can use to foster dual-language learning, regardless of your resources.

The term *early childhood* means birth to third grade. I share the philosophy of the National Association for the Education of Young Children (NAEYC). NAEYC believes early childhood ranges from birth to eight years, because during these years children build the foundation for later academic success. The majority of dual-language learners are in this age group. They are at the beginning of their schooling. Their parents are at the beginning of their own involvement in the formal education of their children. It is a hopeful time and an opportunity to set a positive tone for the future, which is why it makes good sense to support their educators well.

This view of early childhood dovetails with a national education movement called PreK-3rd (Copple and Bredekamp 2009). A PreK-3rd approach integrates the learning experiences of children three to eight years old (from preschool through third grade). Teachers across these grades plan cooperatively and align their resources and instruction to provide an education that's coherent, sequential, and developmentally appropriate from year to year. This movement is gaining momentum as the sciences of child psychology and education become more precise and as educators become more aware of the need for continuity between preschool and the primary grades (Kauerz 2010; Mead 2011). Continuity is especially important for dual-language learners. They must move along the road of language learning and the road of content learning at the same time. If you pay constant attention to the double job of dual-language learners and believe deeply that they can learn, then you will succeed.

How This Book Is Organized

The techniques I propose work for all ages in the span of early childhood. I highlight separate ages when appropriate, but I do not provide age-specific activities. You can plan your own activities—tailored to your students' ages and abilities—using the strategies I recommend.

I have organized this book so that later chapters build upon information in earlier chapters. But you can read the information in an order that makes sense to you. Here's a quick guide:

- Chapter 1 touches on challenges and best practice of teaching dual-language learners.

- Chapter 2 provides answers to questions I hear often about teaching dual-language learners.

- Chapter 3 presents ideas to help you plan a program for dual-language learners.
- Chapter 4 outlines how children develop their first and second language and explains how teachers can enhance this development.
- Chapter 5 offers strategies to support immigrant families.
- Chapter 6 presents tips on setting up an effective environment and curriculum for dual-language learners.
- Chapter 7 discusses how to teach English as a second language in a multilingual classroom.
- Chapter 8 gives ideas for honoring and supporting home languages.
- Chapter 9 helps you assess your environment, instruction, and program quality as well as your students' learning and their families' perceptions.

The examples in this book come from real life. In some cases, I was the teacher. In other cases, I observed the situations during classroom visits. To protect the participants' privacy, I have changed all names and locations.

At the end of each chapter, I offer reflection questions to help you review what you've read and consider your own situation. You can use the questions individually or in dialogue with colleagues. Throughout the book, I provide techniques, checklists, handouts, and tips to aid you in program planning and professional development. An exclamation point icon (such as the one to the left of this paragraph) lets you know you're about to encounter a helpful tip and makes quick reference to the information easy as you do your important work.

Chapter 1

The Educator's Challenge

W hat is the language of instruction?" I asked Mr. P. He worked at
an elementary school where I was observing classrooms. In this
school, most students are Hmong Americans.

"Oh, it's English! But really, we use the language that fits the best
for the situation—sometimes English, sometimes Hmong. It's more like
Hmonglish!" Mr. P. answered cheerily.

Mr. P.'s response seemed sweet and culturally sensitive at first. Then
I looked at the students' academic achievement scores, and I began to
worry.

I remembered a focus group I had conducted for another project at
this school. Its goal was to find out what Hmong families wanted their
children to get from public education. Through an interpreter, a father of
five had said, "I didn't have these opportunities myself in Laos, but here
education is free and good. I hope my children will learn a lot in school,
to get good jobs, so they can take care of me when I am old."

This father's children will not learn enough to get good jobs if they continue their education in Hmonglish. They have a comfortable school environment that acknowledges their home culture. But they're not receiving a good education.

This scenario is troubling because it is common. Educators struggle to teach immigrant children all over the United States. Educators need to focus on this challenge, because immigrant children will soon make up a large part of the U.S. workforce (Fortuny et al. 2009). In this chapter, I will touch on challenges and best practices of teaching dual-language learners.

Dual-Language Learners in the United States

Immigrant children are those born in other countries or born in the United States to immigrant parents. They live in all corners of the nation: in large cities, small towns, and rural areas; in large states and small states; in the West, the East, the South, and the Midwest. Immigrant children currently make up about one-fourth of the nation's seventy-five million children. By 2050 they'll make up one-third of the nation's one hundred million children. Forty percent of immigrant children are three to eight years old (Liu et al. 2008). The majority of young children of immigrants are born in the United States (Fortuny, Hernandez, and Chaudry 2010).

Dual-language learners in the United States have varying needs (Hill and Flynn 2006). According to the U.S. Department of Education (2008), they speak more than four hundred native languages. Three-quarters of dual-language learners speak Spanish as their home language (Planty et al. 2009). Some children live in families with high educational levels, but many children have families with low educational levels—especially those coming from Latin America. This means that their parents may not know English or have the skills to navigate formal schooling. Only 7 percent of immigrant children are proficient in reading at the beginning of fourth grade (National Center for Education Statistics 2011).

The Educator's Challenge

Most immigrant children start their education in schools where English is the main language of instruction. We could imagine that, on average, in a classroom of twenty-eight children, seven are dual-language

learners. In some areas, one classroom might host several home languages. In other areas, large groups of children might all speak the same
home language.

While the details differ from school to school, these facts are certain:
Many educators must teach children for whom English is a new language. And they must teach all the learners in their classrooms.

It's a challenging job. Elementary and high school teachers may get
limited support from an English as a second language (ESL) program.
Early childhood teachers usually get no support. Even with support,
teachers may have difficulty deciding what and how to teach. They
receive mixed messages about curricula and instructional approaches,
little or no training, and few resources. Most educators have good intentions, but their programs have no intentionality.

The first step toward meeting these challenges and solving these problems is to understand them. The following points summarize what educators must grasp in order to teach dual-language learners effectively:

- Educators are nervous about doing the right thing.
- English literacy is the key to school success.
- Educators must teach English explicitly.
- Families need help maintaining their home languages.
- Families need cultural guides to education.
- Multiculturalism is an asset.
- Dual-language learning and teaching are complicated.
- Educators must plan for teaching dual-language learners.

Educators Are Nervous about Doing the Right Thing

The U.S. early education system aspires to respect and protect the home
cultures of immigrant students (Gonzalez-Mena 2008; Copple and
Bredekamp 2009). Educators have discarded the harsh practices of the
past, such as forbidding and punishing home language use. But they're
confused about how to move forward. Emotions and politics sometimes
interfere with practical strategies (Passe 1994; Cummins 2000). Teachers, families, and researchers alike are nervous about doing the right
thing.

Early childhood educators worry about imposing English on their
young students, so they don't teach it explicitly. They hope children will

pick up English and don't understand that the children's real objective is to learn English. Teachers may not know the research on first- and second-language learning—or know how to apply it.

Families want their children to both maintain their home language and learn English at a young age. Families of preschoolers may worry that their children will not learn enough English to be ready for kindergarten. After the children enter elementary school, families notice that their children are falling behind academically. They often try to compensate by speaking English at home, even if they don't speak it well. When the children begin to prefer English over the home language, families mourn the loss of the home language and the deterioration of family communication.

Researchers struggle with their messages. They present educational ideals but do not give concrete suggestions for English and home-language instruction. Nor do they acknowledge the reality of limited resources.

English Literacy Is the Key to School Success

Literacy in the twenty-first century is the ability to talk, read, and write in order to communicate, learn, and work. For three- to eight-year-olds, that means having the early literacy skills they need to be ready for kindergarten and do well in elementary school. These skills are vocabulary, oral language, alphabet knowledge, phonological awareness, and concepts of print (Snow, Burns, and Griffin 1998).

- *Vocabulary* is the understanding that different words represent different ideas.

- *Oral language* is the ability to use words in conversations, discussions, analysis, and problem solving.

- *Alphabet knowledge* is the ability to recognize and name the letters of the alphabet and the understanding that letters are symbols that combine to make words.

- *Phonological awareness* is the understanding that sounds make words and that these sound combinations have meanings.

- *Concepts of print* refers to the understanding that print has meaning and that the words we say are preserved when we write them.

Young children do not necessarily acquire these skills in their home language and transfer them to English automatically. Educators need to consciously help dual-language learners acquire early literacy skills (August and Shanahan 2006).

Educators Must Teach English Explicitly

Teaching English to immigrant children is not disrespectful of their culture when it is done well and explicitly (Lesaux and Siegel 2003). On the contrary: It gives children a skill they need to thrive in the United States—and the world. Affluent children in Asia, Latin America, Europe, and Africa learn English as a second language in their schools. Some families go to great lengths so their children can learn English. For example, one parent stays in the home country, and the other comes to the United States with the children (Cho, Chen, and Shin 2010). They do so because English is currently the world's common language for business, science, and diplomacy. If English is important for children in other countries, then it is absolutely vital for immigrant children in the United States.

Families Need Help Maintaining Their Home Languages

In the past, when communication and travel were slower, immigrants in the United States could maintain their home languages longer and more easily. They may have lived in tight-knit towns or neighborhoods, where many people shared the same roots and spoke the same language—even at school.

The Americanization movement of the early 1900s brought English to all U.S. schools (Young 1991). In the twenty-first century, immigrants plunge quickly into English. English exposure often happens before immigrants arrive in the United States, via the Internet and international television networks like MTV, CNN, and Nickelodeon.

It is hard work to maintain a home language under the pressure of a dominant language. Families need help from educators. For dual-language learners, home languages are the languages of emotions, relationships, family traditions, and cultural values. Home-language support helps families preserve their culture and connections. It also reassures families that their children can learn two languages successfully.

Families Need Cultural Guides to Education

Immigrant families have a lot to learn in the United States. They must figure out the rules of work, shopping, health care, transportation, social behavior—and, of course, education. How does the U.S. education system function? How is it different from education in their home countries? What are the expectations and responsibilities here?

Early childhood teachers are in a uniquely helpful position. They can support families at the beginning of their children's educational careers. They have the privilege of teaching them the ropes. They do so most effectively when they act as cultural guides, not cultural invaders.

A cultural invader says, "Your language and culture are wrong. If you want to be successful, you need to adopt ours and forget yours." Educators may deliver this message with or without words by failing to acknowledge home cultures.

A cultural guide, on the other hand, says, "Your language and culture are valuable. They are a part of who you are. I will help you keep them up. At the same time, I will show you how things are done here so you learn the rules and ways of American culture." The cultural guide acknowledges home cultures and understands deeply that all families share the universal values of love, protection, and nurturance. A cultural guide knows that these values are expressed and lived differently in different parts of the world (Dalai Lama and Cutler 2009). Guides also understand that such differences can complicate their work with dual-language learners and their families.

Multiculturalism Is an Asset

Teachers need to acknowledge immigrant children's multicultural, multilingual experiences from the beginning. Most children of immigrant families are born in the United States (Hernandez, Denton, and Macartney 2008). From birth they hear both their home language and English, and they live in a bicultural world. Teachers should highlight this diversity and use it as a teaching tool. When teachers ignore multiculturalism, they miss good learning opportunities (Gonzalez-Mena 2008).

Dual-Language Learning and Teaching Are Complicated

Individuals can become literate in more than one language. But educators must understand the complexity of language and language learning. Supporting language learning requires common sense, intentional teaching techniques, and hard work. Language learning is a bit like learning to play a musical instrument. A few people can learn to play by ear. But most need careful instruction and a lot of practice to become proficient players.

The demographics of different communities complicate matters. In some communities, children can continue learning their home language in preschool or elementary school. This is possible when children and teachers have the same home language. For example, in some parts of California and New York City, people can accomplish all the business of life—shopping, visiting the doctor, going to movies, eating in restaurants, and more—in Spanish. In many other U.S. locations, however, immigrants come from different backgrounds. Their children attend multilingual classrooms where English is the only common language. The teachers may speak only English or may speak some of the home languages but not all.

Educators Must Plan for Teaching Dual-Language Learners

Early childhood programs and elementary schools must be proactive. To serve both immigrant and nonimmigrant children adequately, educators must create plans that include linguistic and sociocultural goals. They must have solid policies on the language of instruction.

The primary planning question should be, what do we need to do to ensure academic success? In answering this question, teachers identify human resources (staff members, volunteers, and family members); materials (toys and books); and curricula.

Reflection Questions

1. As you begin this book, what questions do you have about teaching dual-language learners? Make a list of these questions and take notes as you find some of the answers in the next chapters.

2. Reflect on the first time you had a dual-language learner in your program. What were your thoughts? What strategies did you use to help the child learn and to support her family?

3. What does the statement "Multiculturalism is an asset" mean to you? How do you integrate this idea into your teaching?

Chapter 2

Frequently Asked Questions about Dual-Language Learning

At the start of my workshops for educators, I ask them what's on their minds about dual-language learning. This helps me gauge what they really need to learn. In this chapter, I'll share the questions I hear most often, as well as my answers, which come from the scientific literature on bilingualism, learning a second language, learning to read, and language instruction.

Is Bilingualism Good for Children?

Yes, bilingualism is good for children. Research has shown that bilingualism improves cognitive skills. Monolingual people don't have to think much about language. One language seamlessly integrates what they know, hear, and say. Bilingual people must be more aware of what language they are hearing and using. When listening, they have to recognize sounds and connect these sounds to a language in order to give the sounds meaning. Then they must decide how to respond. These decisions need to happen quickly. Exercising these skills over and over makes the brain nimble.

Here is an example showing how bilingualism plays out in an early childhood classroom: Five-year-old Marysol enters the kindergarten classroom. She is talking to her dad in Spanish. Her teacher comes over and greets her in English. Marysol smiles and says, "Hey! I am saying good-bye to my dad in Spanish, and hello to you in English!" Then she skips away to join her friends at the puzzle table. This is a normal situation for her, but she understands what she's doing. She can distinguish her two languages, and she thinks that's cool. Marysol is so aware because her family and her teacher talk directly with her about learning different languages.

If bilingual people use both languages regularly, their brains get a lot of exercise. This exercise improves problem solving, phonological awareness, and metalinguistic awareness (Genesee 2007). Metalinguistic awareness is the ability to think about language as a process.

Bilingualism also has sociocultural benefits (DeBruin-Parecki and Timion 1999). It can improve understanding of cultures and the similarities and differences among and between cultures.

Language is a communication tool specific to the culture of a group. A culture has the words it needs for everyday life. Its vocabulary reflects the local geography, climate, foods, and behaviors. For example, it snows a lot in northern Scandinavia. The Sami people who live there have hundreds of different words to describe all the variations of snow they encounter. Another example: European cultures generally dictate that people address one another differently depending on familiarity and social status. So most European languages have formal and informal versions of the word *you*. A French adult, for instance, says *"tu"* to a child or close friend and *"vous"* to an elder or acquaintance.

Children learn the nuances of language through listening, observing, and experimenting. When bilingual children have repeated experiences in both languages, they improve not only their language skills but also their understanding of the behaviors that go with the languages. They develop keen awareness of cultural cues.

Finally, bilingualism offers economic advantages. Immigrants who speak and write English fluently have access to better jobs in the United States (Minnesota Literacy Council, accessed 2012). English is the international language of business (Genesee 2007), so fluency in English and another language is a valuable skill. Bilingualism also improves employment opportunities for immigrants who return home. One Mexican father participating in a focus group explained, "I want my son to learn English well here, because in Mexico, you can have a better job if you can speak and write English well."

What Are Receptive Language and Expressive Language?

Receptive language is the language we understand. Receptive language develops first in the process of learning a language. For example, a baby understands the meaning of *nose* before the baby can say the word. When we ask, "Where is your nose?" the baby points to it.

Expressive language is the language we say. It involves producing language. Expressive language develops in stages. It begins with a telegraphic phase. For example, to convey the idea *This is a pink flower*, a person might first use one word and say, "Flower" or "Pink." Then the person progresses to a two-word phrase and says, "Flower . . . pink." Eventually the person says, "This is a pink flower."

What Are Social Language and Academic Language?

Social language is sometimes called conversational language or basic interpersonal communication skills. Social language is the everyday language of home and community life. "Where is the bathroom?" "It's my turn." "I love you." "Let's go the store." These sentences are all examples of social language. Social language is the easiest language skill to attain. It can be deceptive. Individuals with just social language sound as if they are fluent, when in fact they can participate only superficially in conversations.

Academic language is sometimes called cognitive academic language proficiency. It is the language of learning. It includes all the words we wouldn't hear in daily conversations, or rare words. Academic language involves the use of higher-order thinking skills, such as comparing, classifying, inferring, synthesizing, and evaluating, to interpret what people say. It allows deeper comprehension and participation in discussions. It takes more practice and effort but is essential for school success (Cummins 2001).

For young children, academic language is the language of storybooks. For example, a sentence in the children's book *Annie and the Wild Animals* by Jan Brett reads, "At dawn Annie heard the snarls and growls of the wild animals." This short sentence contains five rare words. They are *dawn*, *heard*, *snarls*, *growls*, and *wild*. At least three of these words would not occur in routine conversations with young children, so children with only social language probably wouldn't know them. If children do not understand these words, the sentence reads, "At . . . Annie . . . the . . . and . . . of the . . . animals." With this level of comprehension, children have a hard time paying attention. When children misbehave at story time, it is often because they do not understand the story (Passe 2010).

Unless they get solid academic language instruction in English from preschool through high school, immigrant children develop only social language. As they proceed through the grades, they can't read the textbooks, understand data on the Internet, participate in discussions, or write research papers. They cannot succeed in school.

How Do Children Learn a Second Language?

From birth to five years old, children learn a first and a second language in similar ways (Bialystok and Hakuta 1994). Young children learn through observation, exploration, and play. If they are dual-language learners, they use the same part of the brain to learn both languages (Kim et al. 1997). Every new object or situation is an opportunity to learn new words and concepts in both languages. From birth to ten years old, the brain is most receptive to language learning (Montanaro 2001). Children who have fewer opportunities to hear and use language learn less (Kotulak 1997).

Older children and adults use a different part of the brain to learn a second language than they used to learn their first language. They use their first language for comparison. For example, they recognize words with similar roots and meanings, such as *revolution* in English and *revolución* in Spanish.

Some research shows that students make better progress in English if they receive schooling in their home language first (Thomas and Collier 1998). But overall, evidence does not support the idea that young children must have specific knowledge in one language before learning it in another language (Wasserman 2007).

According to Patton Tabors (2008), second-language learning follows a predictable sequence involving the following stages:

- home-language use

- nonverbal period

- telegraphic and formulaic speech

- productive language use

This sequence is similar to the way a monolingual baby learns language. The baby listens; points, smiles, and cries; then makes sounds and babbles. As a toddler, the child begins to speak one- or two-word phrases, such as, "Me milk." As a preschooler, the child says five- or six-word sentences instead, such as, "I am thirsty. I want to drink some milk."

Children learning a second language need to know that adults will accept, encourage, support, and expand their experimentations with the new language. Dual-language learners need adults to help them make sense of their new language and improve it, just as when a toddler says, "Truck!" and an adult expands by saying, "Yes, you see a red truck!"

First- and second-language learning can happen simultaneously when both languages are encouraged. A key strategy for encouraging both languages is coordinating the classroom curriculum with suggestions for families. For example, Ms. Molly, a preschool teacher, plans to teach her students about farms and farm animals. Her school's curriculum recommends teaching six new words per week. She chooses the words she wants her students to learn. In her weekly letter to families, she includes the list of words and asks families to talk to the children in their home languages about farms and farm animals. She tells Sara, the school's interpreter, about this plan so Sara can help families understand it. This coordinated strategy offers the children opportunities to talk about an interesting topic in two languages, both at home and at school.

What's the Difference Between Learning and Picking Up a Language?

Learning a language is different from picking up a language (Krashen 1981; Harper and de Jong 2004). Well-meaning teachers sometimes say, "These children don't really need me; they are picking up English on their own!" Learning to speak a language without instruction shows great creativity and resourcefulness. But it is like learning music by ear. Gifted individuals can become proficient musicians this way, but most people need explicit instruction. Similarly, without explicit language instruction, most people develop only social language.

Learning a language is acquiring language skills through explicit instruction. Explicit instruction is showing and telling a child about an object, action, or idea and providing an opportunity to practice talking about it. Without such practice, second-language learners may not progress. They may stay at the telegraphic or formulaic stage. Even if they are able to make social conversation in the playground, they do not develop the academic language skills they need to succeed in their studies.

The following dialogue between a mom and her two-year-old son demonstrates explicit instruction and language learning:

CHILD: Car. *(Points to a car parked in front of the house.)*

MOM: Car! Yes, it's a car. You see a car! *(Smiles.)*

CHILD: Car! Car! *(Smiles and nods.)*

MOM: *excitedly*: Yes, honey, it's a blue car! A blue car! *(Smiles and emphasizes color.)*

CHILD: Bue, bue! *(Beams.)*

MOM: Blue. Can you say blllue? Blllue, like your shirt! Blllue. *(Touches the child's chest and smiles.)*

CHILD: Bue, blllue. *(Touches tummy and smiles.)*

MOM: Yes, blue car! Blue shirt! You know the color blue! *(Kisses child.)*

CHILD: Blue! *(Points to the blue blanket on the couch and smiles triumphantly.)*

This simple interaction contains all the components of explicit language instruction and learning. It includes an affective component: The mom is happy to be with the child and is happy that the child is learning. She shows her happiness and encourages the child in a playful, loving way. The exchange also includes an instructional component: The mother is ready to teach. She makes the new word *blue* meaningful by pointing out the child's shirt. She repeats the word, emphasizing the pronunciation, so the child can hear the sounds clearly. She gently but directly asks the child to repeat the word. Finally, the interaction includes a learning component: The child points to what he already knows, the car. He gets confirmation of his knowledge plus new information about the color blue. He incorporates this information by looking at his blue shirt. When he says "blue" incorrectly, his mother models the correct pronunciation and asks him to try again. He practices. His mom's encouragement ignites his inborn desire to learn. Then he says "blue" correctly and shows that he understands the word's meaning by pointing to the blanket.

You might note that this dialogue is the common way we all learn our first language at home. That's why it makes sense to use the same basic strategies, with the same positive affect, when you teach English to the young dual-language learners in your classrooms and family child care homes (Gillanders 2007).

What Is Code Switching?

Code switching, or language mixing, is using two languages at the same time. Bilingual people may code-switch as a method of common communication (Genesee 2007). For example, a bilingual Hispanic preschool teacher might say to her class of dual-language learners, "Let's go, *niños* [children]! We're going to the park *a jugar* [to play] with *las* [the] balls." She is speaking Spanglish, a mixture of Spanish and English. She is trying to meet the children halfway linguistically. She says some words in their home language to show support and to bridge comprehension.

Code switching shows creativity and depth of ideas. Many bilingual people code-switch in informal conversations with others who are bilingual in the same languages (Pearson Zurer 2008). We do it a lot in our family—any conversation among us might include English, French, and Spanish. Some concepts just have better words in one language than in another. If we know the listener will understand, we code-switch. It's useful and fun.

Code switching is appropriate in family and community conversations. But it's risky in the classroom. Students may get in the habit of using words from one language to supplement the other instead of searching for precise words in one language. This habit compromises their ability to think and speak a language correctly. It hinders their ability to succeed in school. Instead of developing bilingualism (in which both languages are strong), the children may develop semilingualism (in which both languages are weak).

What Can Teachers Do When Children Code-Switch?

A child's job is to learn language. When children learn two languages at the same time, they mix languages because they have some words in one language and other words in the other language. Teachers must accept all their language attempts in a positive way. Meanwhile, teachers must also provide kind, gentle guidance with developmentally appropriate practices. The following examples illustrate different ways in which teachers may respond to code switching. They are not equally helpful.

1. Four-year-old Tomás says, "Quiero más milk." The teacher smiles and says, "Tomás, speak to me in English. You say, 'I want more milk.' In our classroom we speak English! I'll wait until you say it the right way."

2. Tomás says, "Quiero más milk." The teacher smiles and pours more milk into his cup, saying, "There you go!"

3. Tomás says, "Quiero más milk." The teacher smiles and says, "Tomás, you want more milk. I want more milk." Then she pours milk into his cup and repeats, "I want more milk."

4. Tomás says, "Quiero más milk." The teacher smiles and says, "Tomás, you want more milk. I want more milk. Can you say, 'I want more milk'? I want more milk." Tomás repeats, "Want more milk." As she pours milk into his cup, the teacher says with enthusiasm, "Yes, Tomás, I want more milk! You said it in English!"

In example 1, the teacher is inflexible and punitive. Her approach is not developmentally appropriate, even if she smiles. In example 2, the teacher ignores Tomás's incorrect language and misses a teaching opportunity. In example 3, she extends Tomás's language and models correct language. In example 4, the teacher teaches intentionally. She extends Tomás's language, models correct language, gently asks him to practice, and gives him positive feedback. Even though Tomás did not say the full sentence, he learns more English in this example than in examples 1, 2, and 3.

The teacher in example 4 challenges Tomás more than the teacher in example 3. The decision to use one approach rather than the other depends on the context, the teacher's relationship with Tomás, and his mood on that day. If it is a smooth day and Tomás is in a positive mood, she can ask more of him.

What Are the Best Ways to Teach Dual-Language Learners?

Research shows clearly that the best ways to teach early literacy skills are using a thematic curriculum and repeating meaningful activities in large groups, small groups, and one-on-one (Hart and Risley 1995; Dickinson and Tabors 2001). Teachers must provide explicit, developmentally appropriate instruction with many opportunities to practice. These methods benefit all children—both monolingual and multilingual.

In addition, teachers of dual-language learners must tune in to the challenges their students face in a world that's not fully understandable. Teachers should imagine themselves as visitors finding their way in Guadalajara, Mexico, or Bangkok, Thailand, and consider what they'd need to understand and be understood. They must integrate that awareness into all their instructional practices (Jameson 1998). The following techniques have been shown to be most effective:

- using simple but complete sentences

- making gestures

- demonstrating with toys and other objects

- repeating

- following a theme- or project-based approach that offers children multiple opportunities to hear, experiment with, and produce English

If you think about the nursery rhyme "Itsy, Bitsy Spider" from the perspective of a child learning English, you no doubt realize that the child needs scaffolding to understand the rhyme. For example, you may show the child a plastic spider, a picture of a waterspout, or the sun. Visual aids, gestures, and demonstrations support teaching and enhance learning (Tabors 2008).

Children learn language best in social settings, where they can interact with other children and adults to express ideas and understand others' ideas (Dickinson and Tabors 2001). Without such interaction, children miss out on both language development and social development. And when English-language learners speak incorrectly, teachers should resist the urge to bridge communication gaps mentally (Hatch 1992). Even if adults can guess the meaning, they cannot ignore mistakes. Dual-language learners need gentle, direct adult intervention so they can learn vocabulary and syntax and practice talking.

Teachers must also show excitement about language. Children benefit most when their teachers are enthusiastic about language and integrate new words in all their instruction (Jameson 1998). The Early Language and Literacy Classroom Observation (ELLCO) assessment tool recommends that "teachers show their excitement for words through their playful interactions with children." ELLCO also suggests that teachers "model challenging language and acknowledge children's own experimentation" (Smith, Brady, and Anastasopoulos 2008).

Ms. Tammi, for example, has come up with a clever solution to her school's requirement for silence in the hallways. Teachers are supposed to ask the children to "blow a bubble in the mouth" (close their mouths and puff up their cheeks) while they walk through the halls. Ms. Tammi wants her students to use their minds during this time. So she says, "Girls and boys, as we walk to the cafeteria, I want you to think that the bubble is a silent growl, just like the growl of the bear in our story. We won't hear it while we're walking. But when we get to the cafeteria, we can all growl together, okay? Let's go!" The children set out, eyes twinkling in anticipation of the growling. They recall part of the book they just read at circle time. A few let out some muffled growls and giggles. Upon arrival in the cafeteria, they all growl together, experiencing the new word. At the end of lunch, the children ask if they can do the same exercise on their walk back to class. It is clear the teacher helped them get excited about learning language.

Do Children Need to Give Up Their Home Language in Order to Learn English?

In the past, people assumed that in order to develop fully, a second language must replace the first language. This idea is called subtractive bilingualism. Teachers often asked families to stop speaking to their children in their home language. As a result, children usually maintained some receptive language but lost their productive language, and it became difficult for families to communicate.

Educators now know that a child's brain can contain both the home language and English, as long as the child uses both (Tabors 2008). If the child stops using one language, it dries up. Some children consciously decide to use only one language—usually English—because one is easier than two. Some children make the same decision for social reasons, because the home language is uncool. Children are more likely to accept both languages when their parents are bilingual.

How Can Educators Help Children Maintain Their Home Language?

The home language is the foundation for school literacy. Educators must encourage families to continue using the home language at home, while teachers provide opportunities for learning English at school.

Teachers of dual-language learners are more effective when they celebrate linguistic diversity, encourage learning through different modes, and make the curriculum relevant to children and families (Villegas and Lucas 2002). Teachers can show that they value home languages with specially planned school activities. Some examples include:

- using simple phrases, such as greetings, in the home language with both children and their families

- scheduling home-language activities as part of regular classroom routines, such as singing a song in Spanish every Tuesday morning

- sharing the classroom curriculum, such as vocabulary words, with families and inviting them to reinforce those ideas in the home language

- inviting parents to visit the classroom and participate in home-language literacy activities, such as storytelling

- transferring home-language knowledge, such as counting, into English

- consulting community resources, such as elders and cultural associations

Can Dual-Language Learners Learn to Read in Their Second Language?

Yes, dual-language learners can learn to read in their second language. All over the world, many children are schooled in their country's official language while speaking a different language at home. For example, children attend English-language schools in India, and French-language schools in Senegal. In fact, bilingual children may have an advantage over monolinguals in learning to read. Bilingual children seem to have an earlier understanding of words (Bialystok 2001). Some studies have shown that dual-language learners can learn to read in English as well as or better than monolingual English speakers if they receive intentional instruction (Lesaux and Siegel 2003).

A dual-language learner does not necessarily need to learn to read in the home language (Snow 2004). Some evidence suggests that children learn to read best if they get instruction in their home language and in English during separate sessions (Slavin and Cheung 2005). However, if you lack solid academic resources (such as bilingual teachers and high-quality materials) to teach children to read in their home language, it is reassuring to know that you can teach reading in English.

In a study that received the 2005 International Reading Association (IRA) Outstanding Dissertation of the Year Award, Molly Fuller Collins (2005) described how young English-language learners learn vocabulary and new concepts through focused storybook reading. Collins found that having a strong home-language vocabulary was not critical. She explained that three easily implemented teaching techniques were more important:

- reading three times per day

- identifying target words (words that are vital for overall comprehension)

- providing rich explanations

Rich explanations are a variety of techniques that aid comprehension, such as pointing to pictures that support the text, describing these pictures, illustrating actions with gestures, reusing words in simple sentences, and repeating a reading over several days.

Teachers can also reinforce vocabulary and concepts with related activities, such as puppets, toys, videos, puzzles, dramatic play, sensory activities, flannel boards, and other books on the same topic. For example, at the University of Kansas Language Acquisition Preschool, teachers use scripted dramatic play to teach language. They not only provide materials for dramatic play but also introduce the vocabulary, props, and actions formally and engage children explicitly (Bunce and Watkins 1995).

How Long Does It Take to Become Proficient in a Second Language?

In 1983 linguists Stephen Krashen and Tracy Terrell published a book about second-language acquisition called *The Natural Approach*. This book identified five stages of language learning that occur over a span of seven years:

1. Pre-production (the first six months of language learning): Students begin to understand but do not yet verbalize. It is a listening period.

2. Early production (six months to one year): Students have limited comprehension and initiate one- and two-word sentences.

3. Speech emergence (one to three years): Students have good comprehension and can produce simple sentences with grammatical errors.

4. Intermediate fluency (three to five years): Students have excellent comprehension and make few errors.

5. Advanced fluency (five to seven years): Students have near-native ability in written and oral language.

(Krashen and Terrell 1983)

Educators often misunderstand how this process works for young children. Some teachers believe they must "wait it out"—the children will "get it" after seven years. But actually, this information is meant to help teachers understand that learning a second language is an orderly process and that they should tailor their teaching to the learner's stage in the same sensitive way they would be promoting the first language. Their job is to teach actively, providing the right scaffolding—not too hard, not too easy—so children feel challenged but not overwhelmed. For example, a student at the early production stage can answer yes-or-no questions, but not how questions.

Can Educators Guarantee Proficient Bilingualism?

Proficient bilingualism is the ability to talk, read, and write in two languages. Educators can guarantee that children will learn the language they teach in their school. They cannot guarantee that children will be proficient in their home language if it's different from the school language. "Raising a child bilingually in the United States does not just happen—it requires vigilance and persistence on the part of parents and cooperation and continued practice on the part of the child" (Tabors 2008, 136). Proficient bilingualism is more likely when families are highly educated, strongly committed to home-language learning, and have the resources to supplement home-language use with other opportunities. These may include books and videos, trips to the home country, connections with local cultural associations, phone calls and letter writing to friends and family, and weekend language schooling (Pearson Zurer 2008).

Reflection Questions

1. Remember a time when you were learning a second language. Were you a child or an adult? How did it feel? What did you experience? How does your experience compare with the experiences of your students?

2. For you, what are the joys of teaching dual-language learners? What are the challenges?

3. What have you learned about bilingualism in this chapter? What ideas have you gained for your daily work with children and families?

Chapter 3

Planning an Effective Program for Dual-Language Learners

It is August 31. Ms. Cheryl and her assistant, Ms. Mary, just got their class list for the upcoming school year. In two short days, sixteen four- and five-year-olds will arrive in their preschool classroom. The list of names suggests that many students may be dual-language learners. The teachers exchange a weary look.

The beginning of last year was hard. For days, many children cried for their families. Eventually all the children settled into the routine. But they did not make much academic progress, according to the school's new assessment system. Ms. Cheryl and Ms. Mary felt unfairly judged. The assessment did not consider that these children had no experience with school, did not know English, and had families who couldn't communicate with the teachers.

Ms. Cheryl and Ms. Mary felt a lot of pressure—and little support— from the school's administration. The school offered a three-hour workshop by a university researcher, but it left them confused and frustrated. The speaker talked about the benefits of bilingualism and the need to support home languages in the classroom. She explained that children who learn in a bilingual program learn more than children in an English-only program. It all made sense. But afterward they wondered, "What can we do with this information? We have no home-language materials or staff members who speak the children's home languages."

Ms. Cheryl and Ms. Mary are starting the school year feeling defeated. Many early childhood teachers in the United States face similar challenges. They shouldn't have to figure things out on their own. This chapter provides practical, step-by-step guidance for planning a dual-language program in a variety of circumstances.

Planning Is Crucial

After years of evaluating early childhood programs, I have learned that planning is crucial to teaching dual-language learners effectively. Good planning has three key components:

1. leadership that provides clear guidance

2. professionals who work together to plan the program

3. classroom educators who are faithful to the plan

Head Start, a nationwide school readiness program, offers a planning document called "Program Preparedness Checklist." This excellent tool is organized into categories such as program governance, teacher-child interactions, assessment, family partnerships, and several more. If you are with a Head Start program, I refer you to this document. (See Early Childhood Learning and Knowledge Center in Recommended Resources.)

If you are not with a Head Start program, I offer two alternative tools. First, you can use the twelve planning steps listed below to develop and organize your thinking. Then you can use the language planning worksheet included in the appendix to record your language plan. These tools will be helpful for programs or schools with infant, toddler, preschool, and primary classrooms.

Here are the twelve planning steps you can use to develop and organize your thinking:

Step 1: Identify and assess educators' concerns and engage educators in planning.

Step 2: Clarify beliefs about children as learners.

Step 3: Know the children and their families.

Step 4: Identify your goals for the children.

Step 5: Identify your human resources.

Step 6: Provide training for monolingual English-speaking educators.

Step 7: Provide training for bilingual educators.

Step 8: Identify your material resources.

Step 9: Engage families.

Step 10: Decide how you'll use language in your classroom.

Step 11: Develop a strong thematic curriculum.

Step 12: Brainstorm a plan for teaching dual-language learners and supporting their families.

Step 1: Identify and Assess Educators' Concerns and Engage Educators in Planning

Schools often ask staff to teach dual-language learners without much preparation. According to a U.S. Department of Education report, only one-third of educators who taught elementary dual-language learners participated in one hour of related professional development during the last year (Russakoff 2011).

These educators have multiple worries. They worry about how to teach. They worry about how the children will learn. They feel frustrated when they have inadequate resources. Sometimes they feel resentment toward immigrants as their jobs grow more complicated. Sometimes they feel guilt, because they care for the children but can't give them what they need.

It is critical to identify and discuss concerns openly. Afterward, schools can tailor professional development accordingly. And engaging all staff members in planning dual-language programming will create a positive, proactive atmosphere.

Step 2: Clarify Beliefs about Children as Learners

In the example at the beginning of this chapter, Ms. Cheryl and Ms. Mary have to figure out what they believe about children as learners. Every teacher, through formal education and work experience, develops an image of the learner. This image guides the teacher's actions. Some teachers imagine children as gardens. Some teachers see children as builders. And some view children as explorers (Freeman and Freeman 2001).

Teachers who imagine children as plants believe that students will bloom with learning if teachers provide the proper gardening care. The teacher plants the seeds of knowledge, weeds out the bad habits, corrects mistakes, and provides nourishment with new ideas and words.

Teachers who see children as builders believe that students can build their own knowledge by acting on their environment. The teacher sets up the activities, and the children go from one to the next, building knowledge and skills as they go. The teacher is the construction supervisor circulating among the workers, adjusting this and that, making sure the buildings are solid.

Teachers who view children as explorers believe that students discover new knowledge through active investigation. The teacher is the guide who plans the expedition but understands that children already have some knowledge of the world. Dual-language learners learn best as explorers, when they are trusted to use their cultural and linguistic experience. For example, when Ms. Laura proposed that her second graders write a class book about their favorite dishes, the project became a six-week exploration that engaged all the children and their families. The children in her classroom were from Nicaragua, Mexico, Colombia, and the United States. The book became the opportunity to explore language—fruit, vegetables, and meats have unique names even in the same Spanish language, based on the geography—math, science, history, and of course geography. The children brought their background knowledge, interviewed each other and their parents to get new information, and did academic research to complete their learning. The book was in English, as this was the language of instruction, and it was not just a collection of recipes. It was the rich product of a big study.

Step 3: Know the Children and Their Families

Who are the immigrants at your school? Where are they from? What languages do they speak? Why are they here? You have to be curious about them in order to plan services for them. With some information about their background, you will understand their needs better. You will also begin to see the world a bit more from their perspective.

Learn about the Families' Home Countries

The best way to learn about home countries is by researching online. Two excellent resources for this purpose are the U.S. Department of State Background Notes (www.state.gov/r/pa/ei/bgn) and the United Nations Country Profiles (www.un.org/esa/population/publications /countryprofile/profile.htm). These websites provide valuable information on the languages, people, geography, history, economy, and politics of each country. When you research a family's home country, write some notes in the child's file. This will help you remember key facts, such as what continent it's on, what languages are spoken, and which ocean it borders. This information will help you make meaningful small talk and ask intelligent questions. Later you can integrate this knowledge into your curriculum and use it to honor the diversity of your classroom.

Consider Why and How Immigrants Live in Your Community

Try to find out about the mix of documented and undocumented immigrants in your community. The legal status of immigrant families often affects the children's attendance at school. Undocumented families feel nervous about sending their children to school on days they suspect an immigration raid may happen. They may be reluctant to accept services such as special education for fear of attracting attention. Be aware that young children born in the United States to undocumented immigrants are sometimes left here with friends or relatives when their parents are deported. Since the children are American citizens, the parents want them to continue to benefit from the advantages of this country. It might also help them return in the future. Unfortunately, these situations distress the children greatly. This is important for you to know, if you observe acting out or withdrawn behaviors.

Try to find out whether any of your families are transnational. In educated immigrant families, one parent may have stayed in the home country to work while the other parent moved to the United States with the children (Cho, Chen, and Shin 2010). The reasons may be political, economic, or educational. Family separation can bring both practical benefits and emotional drawbacks. The drawback is possible difficulties for the children and their parents to adapt.

Finally, try to find out your community's general attitude toward immigrants. In some areas, immigrants feel welcome. Other communities show resistance or even hostility toward foreigners. In a rural town with a new meatpacking plant, the arrival of African immigrants was a bonus for the school district. The extra education revenue was welcome and even kept it from closing. However, the townsfolk were not ready for this diversity in their community. Being aware of this kind of situation can help you support your students with a positive climate in your own school and advocacy for immigrants in the community.

Know the Children by Connecting with Colleagues

If you teach infants, toddlers, or preschoolers, your school may be their first stop. But if you teach at a primary school, you could learn about the children through a kindergarten transition plan (Passe 2010). I encourage you to connect with the preschool programs in your community, and design a welcoming process for the children to move from preschool to kindergarten. This may happen through regular open houses for families. It could also happen through joint training and exchange of curriculum ideas. Remember that most children of immigrant families are U.S. born. Even with modern family mobility, many preschoolers in your community are likely to continue on to kindergarten. Connect with your community's preschool educators to know your children better.

Use Developmentally and Culturally Appropriate Assessments

When assessing dual-language learners, educators must take care to evaluate cognitive skills (what the child knows) and linguistic skills (the child's skills in a particular language) separately. Let's look at an example.

In standardized language tests, educators show children pictures of objects. The children must name the objects. I am testing five-year-old José in English. I show him a picture of a table. He looks at me proudly and says, "*Mesa.*" I determine that José has cognitive skills appropriate for his age. He can recognize a table and name it in Spanish. Then I go to the next step of my assessment. I determine that José's English-language skills lag behind his cognitive skills. He knows what a table is and can name it in Spanish, but not in English. The language of instruction in my classroom is English, and his goal is to learn English. Now that I know what José needs to learn, I can plan my teaching better.

A variety of standardized assessment tools are available for early childhood. Some are observation tools, and others are timed tests. As the field evolves, more and more tools are developmentally and culturally appropriate. For guidelines on choosing assessments for your program, consult the National Association for the Education of Young Children's position statement "Screening and Assessment of Young English-Language Learners" (www.naeyc.org/files/naeyc/file/positions /ELL_SupplementLong.pdf).

Step 4: Identify Your Goals for the Children

I recently observed breakfast in a multilingual classroom. Each table had several children and an adult. At one table, the adult was a Spanish-English bilingual teacher. Three Hispanic boys, one Hmong boy, and two Somali girls also sat at the table. The adult and the Hispanic children carried on a lively conversation in Spanish, but the Hmong boy and the Somali girls could not participate. One child left the table and got reprimanded. The other two sat silently, staring at their food. This classroom seemed to lack goals for its diverse members.

In my work, I see many good intentions. Teachers and administrators truly want to serve their dual-language learners. They want dual-language learners to succeed. I can feel the hope—but often, I can't see a plan.

What are your goals for the dual-language learners you teach? Think about both linguistic and sociocultural goals. It's important to have goals in order to plan programming and instruction.

Linguistic Goals

Linguistic goals refer to the language skills you want the children to learn. Consider the following important questions: What do you want the children to learn from your teaching? Do you want them to maintain and fully develop their home language? Do you want them to be proficient, at an age-appropriate level, in English? Identifying your linguistic goals will help you plan your curriculum. You can then decide on the language of instruction you will use. Will it be English, the home language, or both?

Sociocultural Goals

Sociocultural goals refer to how children perceive themselves as members of their culture in society. Consider these questions: Do you want the children to develop a positive identity within the English cultural group, their family cultural groups, or both? Thinking about this big picture will help you plan your teaching to develop the children's intercultural awareness.

Sociocultural goals are just as important as linguistic goals. Dual-language learners do not live in linguistic and cultural bubbles. They live in both worlds at the same time. We want them to succeed academically and to feel good about who they are, which means teachers have to consider both types of goals as they plan.

Step 5: Identify Your Human Resources

In an early childhood classroom, the number of educators depends on the number and ages of the children. NAEYC calls for one adult per four babies, six toddlers, or ten preschoolers. This may vary according to state rules. In elementary schools, there is usually one teacher for twenty to thirty children. Head Start recommends that if more than half of the students share a home language other than English, the school should provide a person who speaks that language for the classroom.

Staff quality is important for all children, not just dual-language learners. But programs serving dual-language learners must be particularly vigilant (Espinosa 2010). All classroom staff need training to teach dual-language learners. It's a difficult job with high expectations. Private and public funders, as well as government standards, demand that children be ready for kindergarten. Once in elementary school, the pressure continues for children to be on target for reading and math.

Your plan for teaching dual-language learners depends heavily on your school's human resources. Look around. Who is available, and what skills do they have? How well do they meet your goals? Does your program need to hire new employees who speak specific languages? What training is in order? Look around your community, too. Who could be regular or occasional visitors to support home languages?

Step 6: Provide Training for Monolingual English-Speaking Educators

Good teachers can teach anybody. But teaching dual-language learners requires special strategies and a keen awareness of language (Tabors 2008; Nemeth 2009; Genishi and Dyson 2009; Hill and Flynn 2006). The key strategy is a strong thematic curriculum that integrates learning. Vocabulary and concept development must weave through all parts of the day with talking, reading, and writing activities.

English monolingual teachers need training on language acquisition. When they understand the basics of first- and second-language development, teachers can see the similarities. This gives them more confidence to teach dual-language learners. In addition, the teachers must build knowledge and skills about supporting home languages while teaching English. This will help them strike a manageable balance and have reasonable expectations. Finally, the teachers need cultural awareness training. This will help them understand the experiences of immigrant families, which in turn facilitates working with them.

Training for monolingual English speakers is not likely to be intensive enough until the teachers feel consciously skilled in teaching dual-language learners. After the initial training, teachers will need ongoing coaching to hone their skills.

Step 7: Provide Training for Bilingual Educators

Paraprofessional bilingual employees who work directly with children go by many names. I have heard them called cultural navigators, bilinguals, interpreters, and translators. I recommend calling them bilingual educators. This term affirms their role as people who educate children and families in specific ways, with specific language and sociocultural skills.

In many multilingual classrooms, I meet caring and dedicated bilingual educators. They may be parents of students or nice people from the community.

Some bilingual educators do not know how to spell or read well in their home languages. Others speak in broken English and cannot read English books fluently. In both cases, the educators can neither model nor teach good language skills (Espinosa 2010).

Teaching technique is another common problem among bilingual educators—and it's not their fault. They are typically hardworking, dependable employees with vague job descriptions and little or no training. They're hired to "help the Hispanic [or Somali, Hmong, Ethiopian, and so on] children in our classroom." Without detailed instructions, they follow the classroom routines and speak their home language to the children occasionally. They tend to use home languages to give directions, such as for washing hands or staying in line. Sometimes teachers ask them to translate stories without the use of dictionaries.

It's not fair to give bilingual educators a job they can't do. They may need professional development to improve their English language skills. An excellent resource is your local Adult Basic Education program. These programs are run by school districts or social service agencies. They offer

English classes for adult immigrants for free or at low cost. It is also important to provide training to develop the teaching skills of bilingual educators. Training should include a discussion of their role, which is to use the home language according to a specific plan developed with the teacher. It should also show them how to work with children, with families, and with English monolingual staff. Finally, training should help bilingual educators navigate the U.S. employment system. They are often immigrants themselves, so they may not know all the rules.

The United States suffers a chronic, widespread shortage of skilled early childhood bilingual educators (Laosa and Ainsworth 2007; Mather and Foxen 2010). Many schools can find plenty of willing candidates, but not enough of them with the right skills. To make sure bilingual educators get the professional development they need, I recommend screening their skills at hiring time.

During the job interview, ask a prospective bilingual educator to do two things:

1. Read one short children's book in English and one in the candidate's home language.

2. Write one sentence on a given topic in English and one in the candidate's home language.

If this simple test is challenging for a candidate, you will know that person needs to work on language and literacy skills. You may still decide to hire the candidate because of other important qualities. If so, you should make immediate training arrangements. Well-prepared staff members are crucial to providing good education.

Step 8: Identify Your Material Resources

What learning materials do you have for teaching dual-language learners? Take stock of the available books, videos, toys, computer games, and props, bearing in mind two categories: those for honoring and teaching in home languages and those for teaching in English.

Let's start with home-language materials, using Ms. Cheryl's classroom as an example. Of her sixteen students, five are Anglo (white, non-Hispanic Americans), five are Hispanic from three countries (Mexico, Ecuador, and Argentina), and six are Hmong. I look for materials that reflect the children's diversity. On the walls, I see pictures of children in traditional costumes at ethnic festivals. These don't reflect the daily experience of immigrant children, who usually wear jeans, shorts, and T-shirts in both their home country and the United States. Photographs of the students and their families would better reflect the reality of this multicultural classroom. On the bookshelf, I see books in English and Spanish, but none in Hmong. The classroom library—and the budget for materials—should include all three home languages. Hmong books are more difficult to find, but they are available. Adult and children's dictionaries in English and all the other home languages should also be in every classroom. See the recommended resources for the names and web addresses of organizations that sell books and other materials in many languages.

Now let's assess Ms. Cheryl's English materials. When she introduces the topic of farms, she shows a five-minute video about a farm with pigs, cows, rabbits, and chickens. The interesting show catches the children's attention. Later, when Ms. Cheryl reads a book at circle time about farm animals, the children visualize the animals they saw in the video, and they understand the story better than they would have without the video. Ms. Cheryl understands that students need to see and manipulate materials as they learn a second language. Toys, props, and visuals aid comprehension. Materials are very important. Every item and every use must be relevant and meaningful.

Step 9: Engage Families

Do you know what your families want for their children? Most immigrant families have high hopes for their children. I've noticed that in surveys, studies, focus groups, and private conversations, families always say they want their children to "do better than we did." Families of preschoolers, specifically, want their children to be ready for kindergarten. They know that kindergarten is the first step on the road to a better life.

Do you know what your families struggle with or worry about? Many immigrant families do not understand how the U.S. education system works. They can't judge the quality of early childhood programs. They worry whether their children are learning what they need. As one Hmong mother said, "We cannot tell if a program does a good job teaching our children. We depend on the program and the teachers to do the job right." As children progress through their schooling, families worry when children do not want to speak their home language.

To address all these needs, teachers must engage immigrant families in discussion. Ask your families about their hopes and goals, challenges and worries. Ask how you can help them, and ask them for help in their children's education. Listen to their perspectives, and teach them what they want to know. Give them tips on maintaining their home language, and prepare them for home-language frustrations. View your relationship with each family as a two-way exchange. (Chapter 5 discusses good ways to engage immigrant families and provides an example of a family story form.)

Step 10: Decide How You'll Use Language in Your Classroom

Consider your human and material resources as you decide how to use language in your classroom. What you've got influences what you can do. Language configurations for early childhood programs with dual-language learners include four possibilities:

1. English immersion
2. dual immersion in English and another language
3. English instruction with informal home-language support
4. English instruction with explicit home-language support

English Immersion

In an English-immersion program, children learn literacy and content in English only. The program provides no support in or mention of home languages. If children speak in their home language, teachers simply tell them to speak in English.

Dual Immersion in English and Another Language

In a dual-immersion program, students learn both literacy and content in two languages. This happens more clearly during the formal times of the day, such as during small-group and large-group instruction, and less clearly during the informal times, such as during active learning center times, transitions, physical education, and recess.

The ratio of instruction in each language may vary from 50:50 to 90:10. Usually the ratio progresses from 90 percent home language and 10 percent English to a more even balance as the children get older. The target ratio of most dual-immersion programs is 50:50.

English Instruction with Informal Home-Language Support

English instruction with informal home-language support is a type of program that provides instruction in English with occasional simultaneous translation of books or comments. Practical directions—such as to wash hands, sit down, or go to the gym—are often in the home language. Teachers encourage parents to continue using the home language but do not dictate how. The use of different languages at school is random. When children address teachers in one language, teachers may respond in either language. They do not help the children differentiate the languages.

English Instruction with Explicit Home-Language Support

English instruction with explicit home-language support is a type of program that provides instruction in English with formal opportunities for children to hear and use their home language in greetings, books, and songs. The teacher also provides families with guidance and tools to maintain their home language at home. The program acknowledges and celebrates its diversity of languages.

Step 11: Develop a Strong Thematic Curriculum

Dual-language learners cannot learn language or content with a disjointed curriculum. They need continuity in ideas and experiences in order to learn well. See chapter 6 for guidance on creating a strong thematic curriculum.

Step 12: Brainstorm a Plan for Teaching Dual-Language Learners and Supporting Their Families

Use the brainstorming worksheet to identify your language goals, needs, and resources. What you see on pages 40–43 is a brainstorming worksheet that I completed. You will find a reproducible blank worksheet template in the appendix.

Brainstorming Worksheet

Step 1: Identify and assess staff concerns and engage staff in planning.

Concerns: We do not know the languages of the children. We do not have enough materials in their home languages. Who will help with translation? Who will help with interpreters to talk with parents?

Step 2: Clarify beliefs about children as learners.

After a discussion, the school agreed on this statement: We believe that children can learn two languages at the same time: the language of their family and English, the common language of the United States. The home language is important for children, parents, relatives, and friends to talk, read books, learn rules, and share stories. We support families to continue to teach their home language at home. In our classrooms, we will help children be proud of their home language and culture. We will also teach the children English so they learn to play with other children, talk with teachers, read, and write.

Step 3: Know the children and their families.

By looking at the enrollment forms, we know the home languages: twelve Spanish, four Vietnamese, six Somali. Ten children were born in the United States, eight were born in their home country, and four were born in a refugee camp in Kenya. We need to give parents a questionnaire (let's use the family story form) to get a better sense of what their goals are for their children.

Step 4: Identify your goals for the children.

Linguistic goal: Learn English in our classroom with our excellent instruction.

Support their families to maintain the home language with ideas (weekly newsletter, monthly parent meeting) and resources (books, videos).

Sociocultural goal: children and families will feel accepted as members of our multicultural school community.

Step 5: Identify your human resources.

One English monolingual teacher, two Spanish-English bilingual educators: one teacher, one paraprofessional; one secretary Spanish-English bilingual, one Somali interpreter on contract, one Vietnamese interpreter on contract.

Step 6: Provide training for monolingual English-speaking educators.

Monolingual English-speaking educators will attend two training workshops (September and January). In addition, all teachers who have dual-language learners are invited to a monthly professional learning group to discuss joys and challenges of teaching dual-language learners.

Step 7: Provide training for bilingual educators.

Bilingual educators will attend the training of monolingual teachers. They are both bilingual and biliterate.

Step 8: Identify your material resources.

Few books in Spanish, none in Somali, none in Vietnamese. Will need to buy. Will check with public library to see what they can do.

Step 9: Engage families.

Welcome to families of dual-language learners extended in writing and also personally through interpreters. One-page newsletter will be sent home. Monthly parent meeting with interpreters. Our message for families is "come to these meetings to help your children be good students."

Step 10: Decide how you'll use language in your classroom.

We will provide English instruction with explicit home-language support. This means the language of instruction will be English. In addition, we will have formal opportunities for children to hear and use their home language in greetings, books, and songs. (Schedule to be different in each classroom, based on availability of Spanish-, Somali-, and Vietnamese-speaking adults.)

Step 11: Develop a strong thematic curriculum.

Will develop themes lasting six weeks that incorporate mandated instruction in reading and math. The purpose of the theme is to develop a body of vocabulary to provide continuity for the children. A vocabulary will be sent home to parents and discussed at the monthly parent meetings.

Step 12: Brainstorm a plan for teaching dual-language learners and supporting their families.

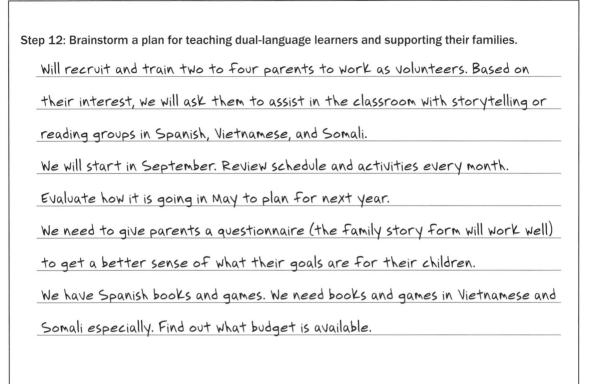

Will recruit and train two to four parents to work as volunteers. Based on their interest, we will ask them to assist in the classroom with storytelling or reading groups in Spanish, Vietnamese, and Somali.

We will start in September. Review schedule and activities every month.

Evaluate how it is going in May to plan for next year.

We need to give parents a questionnaire (the family story form will work well) to get a better sense of what their goals are for their children.

We have Spanish books and games. We need books and games in Vietnamese and Somali especially. Find out what budget is available.

Note: A reproducible template of this worksheet is provided in the appendix.

Now that you've done some brainstorming, you're ready to start planning. The worksheet on pages 45–46 is a language-planning tool. I completed this example so you could see how it may be used. When you do your planning, you will of course include information that fits your situation. The important thing is to take the time to have a discussion with your colleagues and to put your ideas on paper in an organized manner. Incorporating dual-language learners into your overall school plan has to be intentional and explicit. It cannot be an afterthought. This makes classroom language planning very important.

You will probably have more ideas than you can implement. I recommend you start with the most feasible ideas and leave the others for later. The brainstorming you've done gives you an overall picture of your program or school. Now zero in on brainstorming step 10 and work to narrow it down into a specific classroom language plan. Even in the same program, classroom language plans will look different because the student group will be different. In some cases, it may be possible to share staff members, and in others, it may not be.

Reflection Questions

1. What do you believe about children who are dual-language learners?

2. What do you know about the children and families in your program?

3. Review the steps for planning a program for dual-language learners. What steps are you already taking? What concerns do you need to address? Develop your plan now.

Classroom Language Plan

Our Goals for the Children	Sociocultural: Have pride in their home language and culture, pride in American culture Linguistic: Learn English and support home language
Human Resources	Staff language skills: 2 Bilingual–biliterate Spanish–English Family language skills: 8 English dominant, 8 bilingual, 4 Somali dominant, 4 Spanish dominant, 3 Somali dominant Volunteer language skills: 2 Vietnamese, 2 Spanish, 1 Somali All can read and write in home language. 4 are bilingual; 2 are monolingual in home language
Material Resources	Some books in Spanish No books in Somali or Vietnamese Internet access

Families' Language Goals	English: All want the child to learn English well Bilingualism: 20 want their child to be bilingual Home language: None want their child to be monolingual in their home language
Individual Children's Language Skills	English only: 10 Home language only: 4 Bilingual: 13 at different levels of proficiency
Languages in Our Classroom	English for all instruction Every day: greetings in home language Monday: poetry or song in home language Thursday and Friday: small reading groups in home language (Spanish, Vietnamese, Somali) with volunteers and contracted
Our Thematic Curriculum	Our school does not have a prescribed curriculum. We will use the project approach, spending 6 weeks on each theme, incorporating the state standards for reading and math. Each month parents will get a letter explaining what children are learning.

Note: A reproducible template of this worksheet is provided in the appendix.

Chapter 4

Learning and Teaching Language

Seven-year-old Mona and I are sitting on the porch, chatting. She says solemnly, "Last night my dad let me watch a scary movie on TV, and I was traumatized. But afterward we talked about it, and I'm going to be okay." I know how caring and careful Mona's parents are, so the word *trauma* doesn't worry me. Rather, Mona's use of language intrigues me. Ever since she was tiny, she has been talking like a book. She learns big words with gusto and practices them eagerly.

Language development is learning how to communicate. It's a complicated process that includes learning the sounds, words, meanings, and rules of a language. In this chapter, I will explore how children develop their first and second language and explain how teachers can enhance this development.

Introduction to Language Development

Children are wired for language. In other words, children learn language—like walking—naturally, without formal instruction.

Children can hear even before they're born. Babies watch and listen to gather information. The first sound they respond to is their mother's voice. By four to six months, they notice and investigate new sounds. When the telephone rings, for example, babies stop what they're doing to identify the source of the sound.

Babies usually start babbling around five to seven months. Before they can produce words themselves, babies learn that speech has meaning as adults talk to them. Between six and twelve months, babies recognize their names. They also begin to recognize common words, such as *milk*.

Around the same time, babbling becomes more conversational. Babies begin to make noises that sound like speech, such as *mama* and *baba*. The more adults talk to them—imitating their sounds, taking turns speaking to, smiling at, and encouraging them—the more confident babies become in their ability to communicate.

Toddlers begin using one- and two-word sentences between twelve and twenty months. They also learn to pose questions by using inflection: "Kitty?"

Children usually speak in three- and four-word sentences by the time they are three to three and one-half years old. They don't know as many words as adults, but they can use similar grammar. By four years old, they understand the grammar well enough to ask questions by reversing word order.

By seven or eight years old, children sound much like adults. They use correct pronunciation and grammar. Their ongoing language acquisition looks effortless. But actually, adults promote it in direct and indirect ways. When children get a lot of coaching, like Mona, they develop large vocabularies. A child's vocabulary grows continuously through informal conversations and formal learning from books and school (Hart and Risley 1995).

The following chart shows the typical childhood progression from nonverbal to verbal communication. The number of vocabulary words is approximate, and it refers to the words the child understands, not uses.

Language Development

Age	Communication	Vocabulary
Babies (birth–2 years)	looking and listening; gestures; vocalizations; babbling; crying; screaming; spitting; smiling	300 words by 2 years
Toddlers (2–3 years)	looking and listening; gestures; crying; biting; kicking; hitting; vocalizations; 1-, 2-, or 3-word expressions; asking; naming objects	2,000 words by 3 years
Preschoolers (3–5 years)	looking and listening; gestures; 4- to 6-word sentences; problem solving; asking questions; naming feelings; telling stories with a sequence; describing situations; making up stories; joking	6,000 words by 5 years
Primary graders (5–8 years)	looking and listening; gestures; sentences of 6 words or more; problem solving; asking questions; naming feelings; analytical thinking; telling stories with a sequence; making up stories; joking; describing situations	20,000 words by 8 years, learning 20 words per day

For extensive information on language development, consult "Typical Speech and Language Development" at the website of the American Speech-Language-Hearing Association: www.asha.org/public/speech /development.

Children Learn That Language Is a Tool

Children first learn that language is a tool in the context of their families (Halliday 1978). Babies learn that when they cry, their parents appear. From then on, children continue to learn language and use it to get things done. By the time they are four or five years old, children who are ready for kindergarten can use language for these practical purposes:

- To describe things, pictures, or events: "This is a picture of my dad. He is on his motorcycle."

- To express ideas, such as how things work or how to use objects: "All you have to do is turn the knob that way."

- To ask for help when hurt or trying to do something: "Ms. Barb, this puzzle is too hard. I need help."

- To solve a problem, such as resolving a conflict with another child: "I don't want to share right now!"

- To express feelings, such as anger or pleasure: "I'm so happy we are having cupcakes today—it's my birthday!"

- To inquire, such as asking how things work or where they are: "Grandma, how do we make bread rise?"

- To engage in fantasy play, such as being a superhero or playing restaurant: "I am the pizza man! What kind of pizza do you want?"

- To play with language, such as singing or making up jokes and rhymes: "Banana, patana, banana. Hey, I made a rhyme!"

Language as the Foundation for Literacy and Other Skills

Every state has early learning standards that guide early childhood education. These standards include all areas of child development: physical, social, emotional, cognitive, and language. Language serves as a foundation not only for literacy but also for all the other skills children need to be ready for kindergarten and to succeed in school (Passe 2010). Children must have words in their head to describe what they do, what they see, what they feel, what they want, and what they need. Language is especially important in developing social-emotional skills. When children have the language to negotiate and share, they're less likely to bang one another over the head to get what they want!

How Children Learn Vocabulary

Vocabulary is a collection of words within a field of knowledge. Vocabulary is all the meaning that we attribute through language.

The meaning of a word is a comprehensive concept. It includes what the object, idea, or action in question looks like, what it does, what it feels like, what it relates to, what it reminds one of, and so on. For example, the word *apple* conveys the concept of a round fruit that may be red, yellow, green, or a combination of these colors; that has a core with seeds; that starts with pink or white flowers in the spring; that is ready to eat in the fall; that can be eaten raw or cooked; that may taste sweet or tart; that may be crisp or mealy; that grows on trees; and so on. As you can see, just one word carries a great deal of meaning. When a child learns one word, the child obtains much valuable knowledge.

Children learn vocabulary from daily interactions that are concrete and related to their experience. Children also learn vocabulary through dialogue with adults who ask questions, respond to questions, and describe events or objects.

The Stages of Second-Language Learning

Chapter 2 briefly described the stages of first- and second-language learning. Let's look at the stages of second-language learning more closely.

Stage 1: Home-Language Use

When immigrant children first arrive in an early childhood classroom, they usually continue to speak their home language. It has worked for them in the past; they have no reason to believe it won't work now. They are surprised and confused when others ignore them or can't understand them.

Stage 2: Nonverbal Period

Next, the children go through a nonverbal period. Sometimes they point and gesture to communicate. Sometimes they just play silently, alone or near other children. During this stage, children listen to the unfamiliar sounds of the second language and watch for cues in body language, the environment, the actions of other children, and pictures in books. Watchful silence is a smart reaction to this new situation. Teachers must remember that this is an important stage of learning.

Stage 3: Telegraphic and Formulaic Speech

Once the children gather a little basic understanding, they tend to use telegraphic and formulaic speech. Telegraphic speech includes showing objects and pointing, using isolated words such as *juice* or *truck*, and using two-word combinations such as *me play, car go,* and *play house.* Formulaic speech is copying expressions children have heard others use successfully, such as *hey, okay okay okay, pretty good, careful, bye-bye,* and *stop.* Sometimes second-language learners at this stage use repetition for emphasis, with rhythm that sounds like a complete sentence, such as *stop, stop, stop . . . stop.*

Stage 4: Productive Language Use

The final, triumphant stage of second-language learning is productive language. In this stage, children have enough words and useful phrases to build their own sentences. When their attempts generate the correct response, the children are delighted. Their sentences usually have a subject and verb now, such as *I go play, you come; I want playdough;* or *Dinosaur is big!* With practice and scaffolding, children learn grammatically correct sentences and more difficult words. The productive language stage occurs in three steps: speech emergence, intermediate fluency, and advanced fluency.

The Emotional Side of Learning a Second Language

Children learn their first language at home, from their family. Their home language is their emotional language of relationships, family traditions, and cultural values. They understand both the language and the social patterns well.

In the classroom, dual-language learners must interact in a new language. They find it difficult to express their emotions, to feel comforted, and to understand the rules of behavior. They experience both an instructional and an emotional disconnect. They need actions as well as words to bridge this divide. Let's look at three examples.

Ahmed is twenty-two months old. His family is from Somalia. He has four older siblings. His mom has just started a job as an interpreter at the local hospital. While she works, Ahmed goes to a family child care provider who speaks only English. He is having a hard time with separation anxiety.

Mary, Ahmed's caregiver, knows separation anxiety is normal at twenty-two months. Ahmed feels scared when his mom leaves him in a strange place. Mary reassures him in English. She talks to him softly, saying, "I know you miss your mom. She will come after naptime to pick you up." She smiles at him, offers him some toys, and pats his back when he gets teary-eyed. At naptime she gives him his mom's scarf to cuddle.

After one week of this routine, Ahmed begins to realize from Mary's tone of voice and behavior that her strange words are reassuring. A few days later, when he thinks about his mom, he tries saying in English, "Mommy come!" Mary smiles at him. He is not only learning English, he's using it to express and manage his emotions.

Thao was born to a Hmong family in Minneapolis. He is four and one-half years old. He speaks Hmong at home. He does not speak English. He has just started attending a pre-K program. He has been in this classroom for two weeks. At cleanup time, he always continues playing rather than picking up toys.

His teacher, Ms. Julie, wonders when Thao will start following the classroom rules and routines. She can't figure out whether he's defying her or he simply doesn't understand what she expects of him. She knows English is new to him, so she concludes that he needs more time and help getting into the groove.

When cleanup time rolls around again, Ms. Julie takes Thao by the hand and says, "Cleanup time! Let me show you what we do. We put the toys on the shelf. There: I put the truck on the shelf. Good! Now I put the blue train . . . there!" Thao follows Ms. Julie at first. Then he goes off on his own to find the toy plane, and he brings it to the shelf. Ms. Julie says, "You put the plane on the shelf! Yes, you understand!" She smiles at him and claps her hands. She is patient with Thao, and she repeats the message at every cleanup time. On the third day of this routine, he gets it.

Lucia is seven years old. Her family immigrated to the United States from Peru in July. She was a good student in first grade at her school in

Lima. At home, she says she wants to learn English. At school, she does not say a word, in Spanish or English. At the parent-teacher conference, Ms. Katie, her second-grade teacher, is reassured to hear that Lucia talks and plays at home. She finds out that she loves animals of the forest. For the class science project, Ms. Katie proposes to study animals of the forest from the different countries represented in her classroom. Lucia gets to be the expert on Peruvian forests. This opportunity to share her knowledge helps her open up.

Learning New Concepts in a New Language

The other day, a friend suggested that I "Netflix" a movie she recommended. Netflix is a business that rents movies via the Internet. It's popular because it's convenient and easy. My friend could have said, "Rent it." Instead, she said, "Netflix it." This made her suggestion much more specific. She told me exactly how she thought I should rent the movie. I was amused to hear the word *Netflix* used as a verb. And this conversation reminded me that language is forever evolving.

Babies born in 2012 will hear words that may not have existed when their parents were born. The term *cell phone* appeared in 1984, *DVD* in 1993, *webinar* in 1998, and *staycation* in 2005. Some new words come with new technologies, others with changing lifestyles.

The evolution of language is important to consider in the context of teaching dual-language learners. Let's say you teach in a multilingual classroom that includes Hmong children. You've planned a curriculum theme on planets and space. You'll find Hmong words for *sun*, *moon*, and *sky*. But you won't find any for *astronaut* or *spaceship*. The Hmong language does not have words for space travel, because this activity has not traditionally been a part of Hmong culture. Your Hmong students will learn both the concepts of space travel and the words for space travel in English first.

Is this a problem? No. It extends the children's vocabulary and provides understanding about the world. Although the concepts and vocabulary are new and challenging, it would be wrong to deny children the chance to learn them. It is not necessary to wait until the children know the concepts in their first language to begin teaching them in English.

The Role of Adults in Teaching Language

Children are wired for language, but they do not pick it up spontaneously. Language is a social activity. Whether children are learning a first language or a second one, they need constant verbal interaction with adults. Young children learn their first language best when adults do the following:

- Start slowly. For example, the adult uses short sentences and progresses to longer ones. "So happy!" progresses to "You look so happy!" "Truck!" progresses to "Yes, you saw a red truck!"

- Observe and listen to children so you can learn what children know and what interests them.

- Respond when children initiate communication. Imitate the children's smiles or copy their actions. Comment on the children's actions to invite children into conversation.

- Treat children as conversational partners, taking turns initiating conversation and responding to conversational overtures.

- Give positive feedback so children know that they are communicating successfully. This helps children build confidence.

- Wait five to eight seconds after speaking to children, to give children time to think and respond.

Techniques for Teaching Language

To promote language development, adults must teach children skills and vocabulary intentionally. They should use the following specific techniques:

- running commentary
- scaffolding
- expansion
- parallel play or action
- encouragement to produce language
- adding vocabulary

Running Commentary

In running commentary, adults describe what is happening. For example, a teacher might say, "Gloria, it is time for lunch. I am putting strawberries and grapes on the table!" Or, "Ramón, this is a book about insects. It has many pictures of insects. Let's open the pages and look."

Scaffolding

Scaffolding is a technique in which adults ask yes-or-no questions or prompt children to point. For example, a teacher might ask, "Olga, do you like strawberries or grapes?" Or, "Ramón, show me the butterfly. Yes, you are right, this is the butterfly."

Expansion

In expansion, an adult adds to something a child has said. For example, a teacher might say, "Gloria, you like strawberries! I do, too. I like that they are juicy!" or, "Yes, Ramón, this is the butterfly. It has blue wings. Look at the blue wings."

Parallel Play or Action

In parallel play or parallel action, adults engage children by playing or doing the same activity next to them. For example: The teacher joins Tony, who is playing at the sand table. She kneels next to him and starts digging in the sand. She says in a calm and friendly voice, "I am filling the pail. I am putting sand in the pail. My pail is getting heavy." When Tony responds, the teacher continues her running commentary. He learns new words as she talks about Tony's actions and her own.

Encouragement to Produce Language

Adults should give children opportunities to talk. This is especially effective when children have not produced much language but appear ready to do so.

The signs of readiness vary from child to child, but they may include eager eye contact during an interaction, mouthing some words, or pointing persistently at an object or picture that relates to a conversation. An observant teacher invites the child to talk.

For example, a teacher might say, "Lisa, you are showing me the bear. This is a bear. Can you say, 'Bear'? Bear." If the child looks hesitant, the teacher can repeat the invitation and say, "You can say it later, okay?"

It's important to leave an open invitation. Without invitation, children do not get to practice language with adult support. They feel left alone, which is scary to children.

Adding Vocabulary

Teachers should introduce six to ten new vocabulary words to children per week. Children are always learning, so they may well learn more words than teachers introduce.

Teachers need not limit vocabulary-learning opportunities to concepts children already know. Teachers should offer children new opportunities to stretch their understanding of the world.

Conversations should not be limited to formal instruction times. Conversation should happen continuously throughout the day, including during transition times and free play. Even if adults are not talkative by nature, they must remember that talking is their job.

Themes and books are both effective ways to introduce new vocabulary and start conversations. Picture books, in particular, are excellent vocabulary-learning tools. By pointing to pictures, adults can link specific words with their meanings.

Techniques for Teaching Dual-Language Learners

Certain attitudes and behaviors are especially helpful in teaching dual-language learners. I will explain some of them here.

Be Aware of Language

Language awareness is more intuitive for bilingual teachers. Monolingual teachers must train themselves to be more conscious of language. Here are some ways you can increase and demonstrate your language awareness:

- Take a short class in a language of your choice at your local community education center.

- Refer to language throughout the day and in different situations to help raise children's awareness of language.

- Be mindful that language can be a barrier. Augment verbal language with gestures and props.

- Acknowledge the linguistic diversity of your classroom. For example, you might say, "At school we speak English. At home some of us speak English and some of us speak other languages. Sonya and María speak Spanish. Hudah speaks Somali. Ms. Patricia speaks Spanish."

- Honor the languages in your classroom by learning greetings, pronouncing names properly, and learning songs and fingerplays in the various languages. These actions tell the children that their languages have a place in the classroom community and in their education.

Have High Expectations

Children do better when they sense that adults trust them to learn. Children learning a second language are working very hard. They benefit from hearing, "I know you can do it."

Celebrate the Knowledge Children Already Have

Some of your students may not know English, but they have learned many things from their families and their home cultures. This background knowledge is valuable for their future learning in your classroom. First-grade teacher Mr. Mark begins lessons by addressing the personal experiences of his dual-language learners. For example, when he introduces the topic of butterflies, he brings pictures of butterflies, and he divides the children in small groups based on their language. He allows them to talk about the butterflies in their home language. Then he brings them back as a large group and continues his lesson. Mr. Mark realizes the children already have ideas that he can use to expand the lesson.

Show Emotions Accurately

Dual-language learners rely on visual cues to decipher language. If you want to praise a dual-language learner, you can support understanding by smiling and saying, for example, "Pao, you put away the toys very nicely. Thank you!" If you need Pao to get down from the table where he has climbed inappropriately, then you can use a direct tone and a serious expression: "Pao, get down from the table right now."

Pay Attention to Well-Behaved Children

Dual-language learners are at risk of being ignored, especially when they are well behaved. They may sit alone in the block corner or stand at the sensory table for a long time. They appear productive and do not cause trouble. But they're not getting the interaction and support they need to build their language skills. They also miss out on building social skills.

Be Patient

When you converse with children learning a first language, you should wait three to five seconds for a response. When you converse with dual-language learners, you should wait five to eight seconds. It takes longer to think about and compose a response in a second language.

Integrate Learning

You can integrate learning for dual-language learners with a strong thematic curriculum. Explore a topic through language, math, social studies, science, and more. Interweaving study in this way helps children make sense of complex ideas. It provides repeated experiences and lets children make connections between them.

Repeat, Repeat, Repeat

When teachers repeat language, dual-language learners get more chances to absorb and practice it. Repetition need not be boring. Whenever you repeat a word or phrase, you can add a new twist.

Developing the Confidence to Teach Dual-Language Learners

In my work, I find that many educators are anxious about teaching children who are learning a second language. Teachers are afraid to make mistakes. They may also be frustrated that they have to teach students who may require more of their time and energy, when they already feel stretched. They may worry about unfair judgment if the children don't meet learning benchmarks (Freeman and Freeman 2001).

It cannot be denied that teaching dual-language learners takes more time and instructional resources than teaching only English-dominant students. It is simply a matter of being patient, methodical, and aware of language. You can feel confident that you're teaching dual-language learners properly if you demonstrate these critical behaviors throughout the day:

- Listen and respond to children's needs.

- Encourage children as they learn and progress.

- Provide explicit learning opportunities.

- Assess the children's development and learning.

- Work with families as partners.

If you do these things, you can't help but succeed.

Here are some helpful tips for teaching dual-language learners. You can use them as a quick reference for yourself or to train other adults who work with you:

- Read, sing, talk, and write every day with fun and meaningful activities.

- Use short, predictable books.

- Teach and read in small groups of two or three children so the children have more opportunity to interact and practice their words.

- Read the same book every day of the week. Talk about the pictures every time so children have more chances to understand and enjoy the story.

- Teach English words intentionally. For example, when you hand a ball to a child, don't do it silently. Say, "Here, Omar, take the blue ball. The blue ball." This helps Omar associate the words with the object and the action. This technique is called "doubling the message."

- Remember that dual-language learners are doing two hard jobs at once: learning a new language and learning new academic skills.

- Use positive body language.

- Give affirmations.

- Encourage interaction between fluent English speakers and English learners.

- Use running commentary.

It will come as no surprise to you that learning a second language is stressful. A child must pay close attention to the sounds of language and clues in the environment to make sense of what is happening. Occasionally, dual-language learners need a break. Remember that they are learning even while sitting quietly and observing the action. The following tips can help you reduce stress for dual-language learners in your classroom, which in turn will help them function well.

- Prepare quiet areas with pillows, soft toys, and books so children can regroup and observe the classroom without having to interact.

- Repeat activities so children have time to explore and master skills.

- Follow a predictable schedule so children know what to expect throughout the day.

- Demonstrate appropriate use of materials (paint, puzzles, books, blocks, and so on) so children don't wonder what's allowed.

- Provide consistent limits (where to climb, what to do in the various activity centers) so children learn the rules quickly and don't have to guess.

- Model the behavior you want to see (sitting at the table for meals, sitting at circle time, waiting for the bus) so children know what you expect.

- Say the words you want children to say.

- Post photographs of family members on the bulletin board or in cubbies to comfort children and remind them of their moms, dads, siblings, and pets.

Reflection Questions

1. Review the learning standards for your state. You will find them on the website of the Department of Education of each state. Note all the indicators that depend on language and literacy skills. What are the implications for teaching the dual-language learners in your classroom?

2. Choose two children to observe—one child who is learning one language, and one child who is learning two languages. What are the differences in what they say and do? What does each child need from you?

3. Reflect on how you teach. Are you aware of language? How do you demonstrate that? Is there anything you need to change to become an effective teacher of dual-language learners?

4. Enroll in a language class at your local community education center. Keep a journal of your experience. What insights do you gain?

Chapter 5

Working with Families of Dual-Language Learners

Ms. M. brings her daughter Shamira to Ms. Julie's classroom on the first day of school. She smiles shyly and gently pushes Shamira forward, saying something in their home language. Then she leaves abruptly. Shamira bursts into tears.

Ms. Julie tries to console Shamira. Julie is irritated. She thinks Shamira's mother could have stayed a little longer and at least said hello. It doesn't seem like too much to ask on the first day.

Eventually Shamira settles down, but she is very quiet and sad the rest of the morning. At lunchtime her mom comes to pick her up. They leave quickly and silently. Ms. Julie wishes she had connected with them to say good-bye. They left before she had a chance to approach them.

Ms. Julie resolves to be more alert the next day. Meanwhile, she is concerned about how this school year has started. Her new class includes seven dual-language learners. She doesn't know what languages they speak at home or whether they speak any English.

Working with young children means working with their families (Keyser 2006). Early childhood teachers often say, "I love working with children . . . but the parents, that's another story!" It is hard enough to work with U.S.-born families who speak English well. Working with immigrant families is even tougher. In this chapter, I will offer strategies to support immigrant families.

Working with Immigrant Families

Language and cultural differences make it difficult to decipher what immigrant families want, how they feel, and what they think. Some immigrant families seem easygoing, and others seem uptight or defensive. Teachers want to be culturally sensitive and not do anything that might offend. Sometimes teachers feel paralyzed.

Working with immigrant families consists of four key components:

1. understanding them

2. building relationships with them

3. communicating with them

4. collaborating with them

Addressing all four components will help you foster both home literacy and school literacy in dual-language learners

Understanding Immigrant Families

Immigrant families in the United States share several fundamental traits, regardless of education, income, or religion:

- Immigrant families want the best for their children. Around the world, all families strive to love, nurture, and physically protect their children. They do these things differently depending on their circumstances and the customs of their home country.

- Immigrant families arrive in the United States with parenting methods that were successful in their home country.

- Immigrant families want to pass on their culture's values and customs to their children.

- Immigrant families may be new at reflecting on their parenting and school involvement in the way Americans do.

- Immigrant families are interested in U.S. culture. They need and want information and support to help them understand it.

- Immigrant families need educators' understanding and respect for their cultural identity.

- Immigrant families will decide the degree and rate at which they acculturate, or adopt, the customs of their new country. Some families decide earlier than others to speak English, to change their way of dress, or to alter the foods they eat.

What Is Culture?

Culture consists of the beliefs, customs, history, language, and art of a group of people. Culture shapes people's daily experiences, memories, and understanding of life.

Every place has a dominant culture. The dominant culture is the one people accept as the standard for everyday behaviors such as language and manners. The dominant culture pulls in immigrants.

U.S. culture pulls in immigrants even before they arrive. Immigrants often learn about U.S. culture in their home countries through movies and TV shows. For example, everyone knows that the taxicabs are yellow in New York City. The public television documentary *The New Americans* includes a poignant scene in which a man in a Nigerian refugee camp dreams of eating his first McDonald's hamburger when he finally gets to the United States.

A multicultural community of learners and their families may have different beliefs about child rearing. These differences can cause misunderstandings. For example, I recently visited a classroom where a Middle Eastern father had requested that his son not play in the housekeeping corner. He worried that his little boy would learn behavior inappropriate for a male of his culture. The teacher, a man, then had several conversations with the father about the choices they could each make at home and at school. They decided that the family could control play at home, but school was a multicultural learning environment, and therefore the child had the right to play everywhere in the classroom.

Acculturation Is a Choice

After immigrants settle in the United States, they begin the process of acculturation. The first step of acculturation is learning how things work. Small things that Americans take for granted are big things for new immigrants. Everything is new—cooking with a microwave oven, making an appointment at a health clinic, getting involved at school—and everything is an adventure.

Immigrants choose how fast they acculturate. Some acculturate quickly; others take more time. The rate of acculturation depends on personality, education, knowledge of English, and mental health. It also depends on location. If immigrants land in a neighborhood with stores and services that use their home language, they may acculturate slowly. If immigrants are isolated from their home culture, they may adopt the dominant culture faster. Sometimes immigrants participate in specific aspects of the dominant culture for practical reasons. For example, Muslim Somali families do not celebrate Christmas. But they may sign up for a holiday toy giveaway because they recognize the benefit to their children.

Ambiguous Loss

To understand and empathize with immigrants, it's helpful to know that they are probably having mixed feelings about their situation. The immigrant experience is one of incomplete, uncertain, or ambiguous loss (Boss 1999). Immigrants have decisively left their home country behind and are going about their lives in the United States. But they're unsure where they belong. They struggle to fit in here. Meanwhile, they realize they do not belong in their home country either. I recently talked to a woman from Ecuador who came to the United States to study and then stayed on. She said with a sigh, "Eleven years have passed. I don't know how."

Immigrants often leave their home country without formal good-byes. One day they get their papers, and they go. Or they take off in the middle of the night, without papers. They simply absorb the trip itself—the airplane ride, the river crossing, the crowded passage in the trailer of an eighteen-wheeler. Afterward they live with a constant, dull ache of grief and homesickness. The pain sharpens on certain days, such as holidays, birthdays, and anniversaries, or when important family events such as births or deaths occur.

Despite their grief, immigrants are determined to make the best of their situation and to thrive in the United States (Martínez 2004). They want their children to have a better life. In focus groups and interviews, many parents talk about how their hardships are worth it for their children. They mean braving the dangers of travel, being away from family, doing backbreaking work, holding two or three jobs to make ends meet and send money home, and more. Immigrants balance their grief with gratitude and hope. They let go and move forward with faith in a better future (Ogbu 1991).

When we consider the struggles and emotions of immigrants, it's easy to understand why they're sometimes disappointed in their children's education. Educators should hear their concerns as a call to rigor in teaching dual-language learners. Educators cannot be tentative. They must be decisive in what and how they teach.

Learning about Your Students' Families

When I ask teachers what they know about the home cultures and languages of their dual-language learners, the teachers often blush and say they don't really know much. A typical response might be: "I'm not sure what they speak—one of the languages in Africa." Or they say, "They are from a country where people speak Spanish, but I'm not sure if it's Nicaragua or Ecuador."

There are usually two reasons for teachers' lack of knowledge. Either the teachers are not curious, or they are curious but afraid to ask about the families' backgrounds. "How do you ask such a thing? It's so personal," they say. I understand the hesitancy. Cultural information *is* personal. But that's why it's important for teachers to know. When we educate and care for children, we are in relationship with their families.

Eleanor Lynch, coeditor of the book *Developing Cross-Cultural Competence*, points out that "the role of cultural learning is insight" (Lynch and Hanson 2004). Your goal is not to be nosy but to gain insight into your students. In other words, you're seeking information not just to satisfy your curiosity or to add to your own knowledge but to help you teach all the children in your classroom. You need to know about your families in order to honor your students' diversity through your curriculum.

To learn more about the families of the children you serve, develop a family story form like the one that follows on pages 68–69. Or use the reproducible blank template provided in the appendix. Your families can answer the questions either in writing or orally, with help from an interpreter or a home visitor if necessary. Let's look at this example.

Family Story Form

Hello! We are happy that you are sending your child to our school. We are interested in your well-being, and we want to do a good job of teaching and caring for your child. Please tell us about your family and your child by answering these questions. Thank you.

1. **What is your home country?** _Guatemala_

2. **How long have you lived in the United States?** _10 years_

3. **Where did you live before coming to this town?** _Always here_

4. **What languages did you speak in your home country?** _Spanish_

5. **What languages do you speak in your home now?** _Spanish and English_

6. **What languages does your child speak at home with you?** _Spanish with mother, father, grandma, English with brothers_

7. **Does your child speak another language with other people? What language?** _No_

8. **What do you want your child to learn from you and your family?** _To be a good boy, to obey, to be religious, and to have a good job_

9. What do you want your child to learn in our school?   To do math and to learn English

well. To pass all the tests.

10. What parts of your home culture are important to you?   The family love, and to

speak Spanish. Maybe we go back to Guatemala to visit and he can speak

with cousins.

11. What parts of U.S. culture are important to you?   To have a good job, to have many

resources like the libraries, and good schools, and many possibilities for his

life that we don't have in Guatemala.

12. What else would you like us to know about your family and your child?   We are happy

to be in your school. Thank you.

Note: A reproducible template of this form is provided in the appendix.

As you can see from this example, we learn a lot about this family. We know the country of origin, and how long they have been in the United States. The child was probably born here since he is less than ten years old. The parents want their child to have good social skills and to do well in school, to continue to speak Spanish, and to learn English well so that he can be a good student and "pass all the tests." They are grateful for the program, and they are hopeful that their child will participate in and benefit from the plentiful resources in the United States.

Once you have the information generated by the family story form, you will have plenty to talk about. Meet with each family and have a get-acquainted conversation, either directly or through an interpreter. As you chat, you'll find out more about the family's experiences, values, and expectations. You'll discover that immigrant families are not all the same. You'll also notice similarities that will make your job easier.

You can use the information you collect from the family story forms and your meetings with the families to create your own classroom language plan. (Chapter 3 discusses classroom language planning in detail.)

Building Relationships with Immigrant Families

The United States has a low-context culture. In a low-context culture, conversation participants use a neutral tone and controlled body language, especially in a professional setting. We focus on the topic at hand and spend little time sharing personal information. We speak directly and logically. Our behaviors are measured, and we're careful not to betray our feelings. We consider it polite to look people in the eye, say their names repeatedly, and keep a distance of about three feet.

Anglo-Saxon countries, such as the United States, Canada, the United Kingdom, Ireland, Australia, and New Zealand, have low-context cultures. So do Scandinavian countries, such as Norway, Sweden, and Denmark. Most other countries have high-context cultures. People from high-context cultures are more focused on interpersonal relationships, facial expressions, body language, and personal information.

The differences in behaviors and expectations between low- and high-context cultures can cause misunderstandings. For example, when immigrant families from high-context cultures look for personal information and conversational cues from their children's teachers, they often get neither. Families feel they cannot get to know the educators. They then have difficulty trusting teachers, communicating with them, and working together. Educators must take responsibility for learning and using the proper level of context for each family (Lynch and Hanson 2004). The following simple ideas will point you in the right direction:

- Tell about yourself, your family, and your credentials.

- Learn and use greetings in home languages.

- Speak clearly but not loudly.

- Support your message with gestures.

- Allow longer response times.

Tell about Yourself

Many immigrant families will want to get to know you as a person. Most early childhood centers have a bulletin board displaying pictures of staff members, but this is not personal enough for people from high-context cultures. When you meet a child's family for the first time, introduce yourself as a professional and as an individual before you launch into paperwork.

Ms. Paula, for example, has prepared a short introduction to use whenever she meets a new family. She says, "Good morning, my name is Ms. Paula. I am so glad to meet you today! We are going to be working together all year, now that [child's name] is in my class. First, I want to tell you about myself. I have been a teacher in this school for three years. I am married, and I have two children. My son, Ivan, is eight. My daughter, Sara, is five. I have a degree in teaching from the University of Minnesota."

A simple introduction like Ms. Paula's satisfies a family's curiosity about you immediately. When you tell about yourself, your family, and your credentials, you create a context for yourself and establish a personal relationship with the family. This personal connection paves the way for professional questions and discussions about the family's child or your curriculum.

Learn and Use Greetings in Home Languages

Saying hello in Hmong, Swahili, or French is a friendly way to connect with the children and families who come into your room. The children's book *Hello World! Greetings in 43 Languages* by Manya Stojic is a great resource. If you are not sure how to pronounce a greeting, show it to a family who speaks that language or to your interpreter and ask how to say it correctly. This simple act will show families that you are willing to learn from them.

Speak Clearly but Not Loudly

Because I speak English with an accent, strangers often talk to me very loudly at first. It is a natural reaction to hearing me. I know they just want to help me understand them. Sometimes it's amusing, and sometimes it's irritating.

Be aware of this tendency and work to control it. Speaking louder does not make words more understandable. However, speaking slowly and using plain language does help. Speak clearly but not loudly. For example, instead of shouting, "Today Pao progressed in his small-motor skills!" say in a softer voice, "Today Pao cut paper with scissors for a long time. That is good exercise for his fingers. It will help him learn to write."

Support Your Message with Gestures

When you're talking to Pao's family about his work with scissors, you can help them understand by making a cutting gesture with your index and middle fingers. Gestures and exaggerated facial expressions are effective ways to increase comprehension. Tourists use these methods un-self-consciously when they're traveling in a foreign country. Remember that teaching in a multilingual classroom is like taking an international trip. Feel free to point, nod, gesture, and act out your words. Immigrant children and families will appreciate the support.

Allow Longer Response Times

A person learning a new language needs a five- to eight-second response time during conversations in that language. This is much longer than a fluent speaker needs. Try to get comfortable with this silent time, because it is valuable. Remember that when you're talking with immigrant families, they aren't listening passively; they're actively deciphering language and formulating a reply.

Communicating with Immigrant Families

In the United States, language assistance is guaranteed under Title VI of the Civil Rights Act of 1964. By law, institutions that receive federal funds must provide the services of a qualified interpreter to clients who are not fluent in English. This law is meant to ensure that everyone has equal access to public services such as hospitals and schools. The interpreter's services must be provided at no cost to the patient or client. The organization may choose what kind of interpretation service to provide.

It may provide a professional interpreter, a bilingual employee, or a telephone interpreting service. The law allows a reasonable amount of time if an interpreter cannot be found immediately. It also allows the patient or client to have an adult friend or relative interpret. However, the law prohibits anyone under eighteen years old from serving as an interpreter in this capacity.

Communicating through an Interpreter

The job of a school interpreter is to translate language orally during formal meetings and informal interactions between staff and immigrant families. Early childhood programs and elementary schools do not usually have clear guidelines or job descriptions for interpreters. It's hard to find professionals who are equally skilled in English and their home language, have formal training as interpreters, and have knowledge of child development and early childhood education. The typical interpreters in schools and social service agencies are kind, well-meaning individuals from the community doing the best they can with little guidance and few resources. The following tips will help you plan for language interpretation in your program.

Before the family meeting:

- Select an appropriate interpreter.
- Make sure the interpreter is an adult who is fluent in English and in the home language.
- Meet with the interpreter.
- If you are having a one-on-one meeting with an interpreter of the opposite sex, be aware of gender-related social customs in the interpreter's home culture.
- Make sure the interpreter is well versed on the topic to be discussed with families. If necessary, give the interpreter materials to aid preparation.
- Answer the interpreter's questions and explain important concepts.
- Give the interpreter the same documents you will share with families.

During the family meeting:

- Allow more time for a multilingual meeting than you would for a monolingual meeting. Stay focused on the most essential information. Interpreting takes a lot of energy and time.

- Arrange the seating in a triangle or circle, depending on the size of the group.

- At the beginning of the meeting, let the interpreter give a self-introduction and explanation of the interpreter's role.

- Explain the ground rules for the meeting:

  - All personal comments made about children, family members, and staff are confidential.

  - One person at a time should speak.

  - Use short speech segments with frequent pauses.

  - Raise a hand to indicate the need for clarification, then ask the question.

  - If the interpreter needs to ask a clarifying question, the interpreter should say, "I need to ask a clarifying question."

- Speak clearly and simply. Avoid jargon, slang, or jokes.

- Use visual aids that relate directly to your words.

- Use PowerPoint only to show pictures that illustrate important concepts. For example, if you're giving a presentation on child development, you might show slides of different-aged children playing with appropriate toys. Do not use slides with words.

- Plan for breaks every forty-five minutes.

- Do not ask the interpreter for personal opinions during the meeting. Do not look at the interpreter unless you're speaking directly to the interpreter.

- Maintain eye contact with the audience while you are speaking and while the interpreter is speaking. This strategy helps you make connections and gauge reactions.

At the end of the family meeting:

- Check with the family or group to see if they understood you.

- Summarize key points and next steps.

- Immediately after the family or group leaves, review the meeting with the interpreter.

Communicating in Writing

In our work as educators, we often use educational jargon, the specialized language of education. For example, we speak of early literacy skills, approaches to learning, manipulatives, or large-motor equipment. We have a lot of educational knowledge and experience, so we know exactly what these terms mean. We can picture children learning to talk, read, and write and children being excited about learning. We can imagine puzzles and Lego blocks and children playing on ladders and slides. But most families do not have our educational knowledge and experience. When we use jargon, families often do not understand what we're saying.

Educational jargon is even harder to understand in a second language than in a first language (Passe 2010). And when we translate jargon directly from English into a home language, it becomes incomprehensible. Some languages, like Hmong and Somali, have limited vocabulary for modern scientific early childhood education. I see many meaningless translations of educational standards, developmental scales, and assessments into Spanish and French. My colleagues who are fluent in other languages see similar problems. Meaningless translation defeats the purpose of translation. Avoid using educational jargon in your written communication with immigrant families.

On October 13, 2010, President Barack Obama signed the Plain Writing Act. Its goal is to make government documents easier to understand by using simple and clear language. You can find valuable information about this law and about plain language at www.plainlanguage.gov. Plain language—both in English and in translation—is particularly important for teachers who work with immigrant families. If we give parents materials that are too difficult to understand, our efforts are wasted. We do not achieve the goals of informing parents accurately. We also discourage parents from being meaningfully engaged in their children's education. They feel intimidated and inadequate.

Get in the habit of checking the readability level of your written materials. Various computer tools can be helpful in checking the readability of documents in terms of plain language. Microsoft Word, for example, has a tool called Readability Check, which you can find by clicking the question icon for Word Help. Another option is to use Renaissance Learning's online readability analyzer at www.renlearn.com /ar/overview/atos.

Both of these tools are connected to the Spell Check function and will tell you the approximate grade level of reading difficulty for the text.

For example, if the result is 10.4, this means that the reading difficulty is between tenth and eleventh grade. As a reference, think that newspaper articles are usually written at the eighth-grade level.

For most information directed at immigrant families, I recommend writing at a fourth- to eighth-grade reading level. At first, you will find it difficult to lower the readability of your documents. You might worry about leaving out crucial information. Rest assured that it's far better to provide simplified information than comprehensive information in language that's too difficult to understand.

I recommend that you use the Plain Language website as a resource. It gives many useful suggestions and a complete vocabulary list to transform jargon into plain language. For example, it suggests substituting words like *women* for *females*, *help* for *assistance*, or *move* for *relocate*. Go to www.plainlanguage.gov.

Following is an example of a text written in educational jargon at an eleventh-grade reading level. The text is an excerpt from the *Early Childhood Indicators of Progress: Minnesota's Early Learning Standards* (Minnesota Department of Education 2005, 44):

> Children show progress in mathematical and logical thinking when they:
>
> - Demonstrate increasing interest in and awareness of numbers and counting.
> - Recognize and duplicate simple patterns.
> - Use words that show understanding of order and position of objects.
> - Use simple strategies to solve mathematical problems.

The following is the same text translated into plain English at a sixth-grade reading level:

> We can see that children are learning about math when they:
>
> - Show interest in numbers and counting.
> - Notice patterns of colors or shapes and can make their own patterns.
> - Use words like *first*, *second*, *before*, and *after* to describe where objects are.
> - Begin to solve math problems, such as deciding if four napkins are enough when five children are at the table.

When you write for readers with low English literacy skills:

- Use plain English.

- Use active voice and a conversational style.

- Use short sentences.

When you format documents for readers with low English literacy skills, try to also keep it simple and straightforward:

- Use a large typeface (larger than 12 point) for text. Use an even larger typeface for headings.

- Use a lot of white space around articles and stories to clearly separate them.

- Use illustrations to complement the text—not just to decorate it.

Translating complex information into plain language benefits not only families but also educators. It forces us to think deeply about what we're doing. For example, if we can't explain to children and families what the students are learning, then how do we know what we are teaching? How do we know we're using the right methods and materials to achieve our goals?

Once you've got your written materials in plain English, the next step is to translate them into the appropriate home language. Enlist a translator who is fluent and literate in both languages. Do not use an automatic computer translator. At best it will produce humorous text that conveys the gist of your message. At worst it will produce misleading or incomprehensible text.

When you translate or have materials translated for immigrant families:

- Review the original English material. Look for educational jargon and other academic or otherwise complex language.

- Convert the complex English to plain English.

- Translate the plain English into the home language.

Collaborating with Immigrant Families

When I present workshops for staff who work with dual-language learners, I often do an exercise I call "Exploring the Grand Canyon." I ask the participants to imagine that they're planning a trip to the bottom of the Grand Canyon, and they need to hire a guide. The Grand Canyon is big, beautiful, and impressive. At the same time, it's dangerous, mysterious, and scary. It serves well as a symbol for the United States.

I ask the participants to start by summarizing their feelings about hiking down into the Grand Canyon. They often say things like, "I feel scared and sometimes panicked. I feel excited, nervous, and in awe."

Then I ask the participants what they want from a Grand Canyon guide. They usually say they need a guide who will be:

- informative about the area's history

- competent

- experienced

- affordable

- prepared for the unexpected

- respectful of them and their lack of experience

- accepting

- confident

- bilingual

- understanding and patient with the many questions they will ask

- aware of the different capabilities of the group's individuals

- trusting that they will do well

- punctual and dependable

- fun and friendly

And they say they need a guide who will:

- teach them safety precautions and keep them safe

- smile, have fun, and show a sense of humor

- avoid being grumpy

- make the experience enjoyable for everyone

- tell them the plan, including what will happen and what they'll see

- give clear instructions

- prepare them for the environment with the appropriate equip-ment, information, and survival skills

- have patience

- make them feel comfortable in an unfamiliar situation

- take care of them

- respond to their different personalities and deal with unexpected reactions

In many ways, the U.S. immigrant experience resembles a trip to the Grand Canyon. When immigrants travel to the United States, they have great hope. They want the best for their families. They are simultaneously excited and scared, nervous and awestruck by the newness and the possibilities. They want to fit in, and they want to learn how to do so. They miss their home and its ways, but they also like some of their new experiences.

As educators, your responsibilities are similar to those of a Grand Canyon guide. You must give information to families in ways that help them understand their importance and face their work confidently. This information must be clear and direct. It should spell out benefits as well as consequences. Educators must exercise empathy and understanding and avoid judgment (Barrera and Corso 2003).

Educators as Cultural Guides

The U.S. concept of families' involvement in their children's schools has evolved greatly over the past thirty years. Schools expect more from families today. U.S.-born families are used to this level of involvement, but immigrant families typically aren't. In addition, immigrants must learn the norms of family involvement in U.S. schools.

For example, many teachers put newsletters, flyers, completed projects, permission slips, report cards, and other information in a special communication folder that children carry back and forth in their backpacks. Parents are expected to read all the information—and complete and return items that require a response—within a certain number of days. This process is familiar and easy for U.S.-born educators and families. For immigrant families, it is new and requires explanation.

I once taught in a program that asked parents to supply beverages for the children's snacks. The program newsletter specified that snacks and beverages should be healthy. When an immigrant family provided orange soda, my colleagues were horrified at first. They anguished over how to handle the situation. Then they realized it was a teachable moment about the difference between orange soda and orange juice. Over the next few weeks, the teachers, children, and families explored how to make healthy eating decisions in a land of abundance.

Encouraging Immigrant Families

In 1995, Elizabeth Hart and Todd Risley published research showing big differences in the type and amount of language and literacy experiences young children get at home. In college-educated families, children begin the literacy process as babies, when their parents read books to them. The process continues as the parents ask their toddlers open-ended questions to stimulate their thinking and as they respond to their preschoolers' endless questions with patient encouragement. A child in a highly educated family will hear eleven million words per year.

Children in families with low educational levels, on the other hand, get less reading time and fewer conversations and questions. They also get fewer opportunities for verbal problem solving and less praise for their achievements. A child in a family with a low educational level will hear only three million words per year.

We know that children's ability to read depends on their oral language development and the size of their vocabulary. We also know that children acquire vocabulary when adults talk and read to them. So by the time children get to kindergarten, a gap already exists in their chances for school success.

Teachers who work with English-language learners in families with low educational levels must keep this research in mind. It's important to the children's academic future. We must help families understand their value in developing their children's literacy. The most important thing they can do is to talk with their children in their home language. Meanwhile, we must also reassure families that while they do their job, we will do ours: teaching their children English.

Immigrant families already know that literacy is the key to success, and they want to help their children become literate. A few years ago, I conducted focus groups with new immigrant families. I asked them, "What is literacy?" and, "What does literacy mean to you?" Here are some of their responses:

- "Reading is important to get a good education so they [my children] can support themselves so they don't depend on their parents."
- "Reading is good to understand new things."
- "In my country I cannot be educated, but here I can be. There is freedom to be educated with books."
- "Reading is good for the mind. It makes you think differently."

- "Reading to kids, we can teach them about real life. If the boy in the story is naughty, we can talk about it and tell our child not to be naughty like that boy."

- "Reading is good to learn English."

Educators can help make the journey to literacy easier for immigrant families and open the door to success in our society.

Home Language as a Foundation for School Literacy

The home language is the language that builds emotional bonds and connects people to their culture of origin. Immigrant families with a high level of education are fully literate in their home language. Immigrant families with a low level of education may have only oral literacy in their home language.

When families use only their home language at home, children learn concepts and vocabulary in that language. When families are bilingual, children learn concepts and vocabulary in both languages.

When immigrant children begin to learn English, whether they are learning it at home or at school, English becomes a key part of their cultural connection to the United States. Children learn that there are two languages: the language of home and the language of the community. Both languages are important for full participation in U.S. society.

Bridging Home and School Literacy

Amina is four years old. Her parents are Somali immigrants. Her father works as a janitor, and her mother is a full-time homemaker caring for their three young children. Amina's parents cannot speak or read English fluently. A Head Start teacher tells Amina's parents that they should read to her at home to help her be ready for kindergarten. They want Amina to succeed in school, but they don't know what to do.

In our highly literate society, encouraging families to "just read" to their children seems like a simple request. And we have good reasons for making it. Reading only fifteen minutes per day makes a big difference in a child's learning. Research shows that reading to children helps them develop literacy skills and a love of books. It also shows that oral language skills and a large vocabulary are necessary for learning to read. When children have many words and concepts in their heads, they can understand the stories and ideas presented in books, and they can ask questions to learn more.

Educators sometimes don't realize that for adults with low literacy and familiarity with books, it's hard to "just read." Even talking about the pictures in a book can be difficult. Teachers often neglect to offer alternative strategies. Families want the best for their children, and they end up feeling instead as if they're failing their children.

What can Amina's teacher and parents do? Amina's teacher knows that literacy is the ability to talk, read, and write, which enables communication, learning, and work. The teacher should explain that the more adults talk, read, and write with young children, the better they prepare the children for life in school and in society.

Amina's parents should focus on the talking part of literacy. The teacher should assure them that they already know information that will be immensely valuable to Amina's education. They have a rich background of life experiences and traditional stories that they can talk about with Amina. Conversations in their home language will fill Amina's head with words and concepts.

For example, if Amina's parents talk with her in Somali about *shimbiro* (birds), she learns that a bird has feathers, a beak, and two legs; that most birds fly; and that they can be many colors. Later, Amina's teacher reads a story about birds. Amina already knows what birds are. She has a concept of birds in her brain, and she also has Somali words to describe birds. She just needs to learn the words in English. This is a simpler task than learning the concept of birds, the words in English, and the words in Somali.

When teachers communicate with immigrant families, they should remember that it may not be possible for parents to read to their children. Every time teachers talk with families, they should make a point of telling families how important they are to their children's education. Families need to know that when they talk to their children in their home language, they are helping the children become literate and learn English. The path to literacy begins at home in the home language, and it continues at school.

Encouraging Families to Maintain Their Home Language

Immigrant families want their children to learn English, but they also want the children to maintain their home language. This isn't an easy job. It's especially difficult for families with a low level of education. Adults with low educational levels tend to have low-paying jobs, and they often hold multiple jobs. They find it hard to spend much time conversing or playing with their children. Their talk consists mostly of caretaking statements.

But even in difficult circumstances, families can help their children maintain their home language. In the parent handout that follows, I offer tips for encouraging immigrant families. You can share these with families orally or in writing.

Parents, You Can Help Your Children Be Bilingual!

Keeping up your home language in a new country is not easy. You must work hard at it and not give up. Sometimes children want to speak their home language. Sometimes they do not. It depends on their interest, their personality, and their ability.

You need to have a plan. With planning and effort, you can help your children be bilingual. Your children may not appreciate this gift now, but they will be grateful when they are older. Their thanks will be a nice reward for you.

Here are some tips to keep up your family's home language:

- **Talk with your children all the time.** Talk with your children about everything that happens during the day. You can talk about what to cook for dinner. You can talk about visiting a friend on the weekend. You can talk about a book or magazine article you have read. Speak in your home language even if your children respond in English. If you keep speaking in your home language, your children will continue to understand it.

- **Have a system.** Make a rule about how your family will use your home language and English. This will help your children know what to expect. For example, you might:

  - Speak your home language at home and English at school.

  - Speak your home language at home and English outside your home.

  - Speak your home language with one parent and English with the other parent.

- **Find other people who can speak your home language with your children.** For example, you might:

  - Gather with friends and relatives who live in your community. Go to parties, religious events, or traditional celebrations.

  - Interact with friends and relatives who live in your home country. You can talk to them on the phone. You can also exchange letters and e-mail messages.

- **Visit your home country.** If this is possible, it will immerse your children in your home language. After just a few days in your home country, your children will understand and speak more words in your home language.

- **Set a good example.** If you are bilingual, your children will think it is natural to be bilingual. They will be more interested in both languages.

Note: A reproducible template of this handout is provided in the appendix.

Training Families to Volunteer in the Classroom

Many early childhood programs invite family members to work in the classroom as volunteers. But many people simply don't know how to be helpful in the classroom, even if they have small children at home. Head Start recommends that schools provide training to families to show them how to be helpful.

The challenge is even greater for immigrant families. They may feel inadequate because they do not speak English well. Or they may not be familiar with American educational practices, and not know how to act in our classrooms. But the rewards of spending time in the classroom are valuable. Families can promote home-language development through volunteering in the classroom to share songs, stories, and conversation with the children (Office of Head Start 2010).

It is the job of educators to structure what volunteers do and to support them. The goal is to make it a positive experience so they can be truly helpful. I propose that you offer a workshop for your families. Hold the workshop in the classroom so volunteers become familiar with the space and the materials. Here's a plan you can use to train families or other volunteers from the community:

1. Invite volunteers to a one-hour training session.

2. Explain the classroom schedule (arrival, mealtimes, large group, small group, active learning, outdoor play) with the help of pictures.

3. Explain that children learn literacy by talking, reading, and writing in English and in their home language. Since you do not speak their home language, you are grateful for the volunteers' help.

4. Explain that talking helps children learn words. Learning words is an important step toward learning to read.

5. Let volunteers know they won't be responsible for a group of children until they've had more experience in your classroom.

6. Choose three areas where volunteers could help, and demonstrate what they could do. For example, you could ask them to do the following:

   ○ Sing a song, tell a story, or read a book in their home language to a large or small group of children.

   ○ Sing songs, read books, or tell stories to individual children.

   ○ Play and talk in their home language in the dramatic play area or in the library area.

   ○ Sit and eat with children while talking with them in their home language.

7. Give volunteers a chance to ask questions and time to explore the classroom.

When volunteers report for duty in the classroom, ask them what they prefer to do and give them choices. You will notice that volunteers, including immigrant parents and community members, become more confident and more useful as time passes. This generates good feelings for them personally. It also creates a positive reputation for your school or program as a good place for their children.

Assessing Your Program's Family Support

How well do you work with the families of dual-language learners? Fill out the following checklist to assess your program's strengths and weaknesses. This will help you identify the areas where you excel as well as the areas where you can do more.

Essential Elements for Family Support

Essential Elements	Always	Sometimes	Never
Educators explain to families the process of second-language learning and bilingualism.			

Essential Elements	Always	Sometimes	Never
Teachers explain to families the role language plays in academic success.			
Educators teach families how to maintain the home language at home.			
Before a curriculum unit begins, teachers share key vocabulary and concepts with families in English and home languages.			
Educators deliver information about the school and the children in English or home languages as necessary.			
Teachers provide information on how to support children's bilingualism at home.			
Educators share children's assessments with their families.			
Teachers help children and families navigate the U.S. educational system.			
The school is family friendly, with signs and materials in plain English or translated into plain language, culturally competent staff, and interpreters when needed.			

Note: A reproducible template of this handout is provided in the appendix.

Reflection Questions

1. How do you interpret your role as a cultural guide for immigrant families?

2. Complete the Essential Elements for Family Support checklist. What items are you already doing? What items do you need to work on?

3. Write your own letter to families encouraging them to use their home language at home.

Chapter 6

Environment and Curriculum for the Multilingual Classroom

In this chapter, I want to help you bridge the gap between the ideal and the real, the impossible and the possible. You have an important and difficult job, and I want to help you make it manageable. This chapter will focus on two areas: the classroom environment and the curriculum that are most effective for teaching dual-language learners. It will address how to honor home languages as part of your curriculum and daily routines, whether you teach infants, toddlers, preschoolers, or primary graders.

Planning and Managing the Dual-Language-Learning Environment

Children may spend up to ten hours per day in a child care center or home. They may spend up to six hours per day in a preschool or elementary school. In a classroom set up with care, teachers should be able to answer "yes" to these five questions:

1. Is the child safe?

2. Can the child see who she is?

3. Does the child hear the language of his community and the language of his family?

4. Does the child have the right materials to learn in the best way?

5. Does the child feel calm, not overstimulated?

These questions are, of course, applicable to all environments. But let's think about them as they apply to the dual-language learning environment.

Is the Child Safe?

Every early childhood space should be free of dangers and open for exploration in a way that is developmentally appropriate for all the children who inhabit it. The following resources can help you set up a nurturing and safe early childhood environment:

- *The Creative Curriculum for Family Child Care* by Diane Trister Dodge, Sherrie Rudick, and Laura J. Colker

- *The Creative Curriculum for Infants, Toddlers and Twos* by Diane Trister Dodge, Sherrie Rudick, and Kai-leé Berke

- *The Creative Curriculum for Preschool* by Diane Trister Dodge, Laura J. Colker, and Cate Heroman

- *Designs for Living and Learning: Transforming Early Childhood Environments* by Deb Curtis and Margie Carter

- *Developmentally Appropriate Practice in Early Childhood Programs* by Carol Copple and Sue Bredekamp

Can the Child See Who She Is?

Children need to see themselves represented in their environment. This is especially true for immigrant children, because they may look different from the mainstream culture, so they may feel isolated. Commercial posters and pictures of children around the world in traditional dress do not accomplish this. Colorful, festive costumes do not accurately reflect the daily lives of real immigrant children—either here or in their home country. Here are some ideas to help you reflect in your environment the diversity of your students:

- **Post pictures of your students at home and with their families.** The pictures should reflect the topic you are currently studying. For example, if you are studying food, you might ask for pictures of the children at home cooking with their moms, dads, or grandparents. If you are studying transportation, you might ask for pictures of the children with their bikes, in their cars or trucks, or riding the bus.

- **Post drawings and paintings made by your students.** Each piece of artwork should bear a title or a comment dictated by the child. The writing may be in English, in the home language, or in both.

- **Select fiction and nonfiction books carefully.** Choose books with photographs or illustrations that reflect the diversity of all the children in your classroom. (See Recommended Resources for websites where you can find books in rare languages.)

- **Make your own classroom books.** The children and their families can be the main characters.

- **Mount mirrors on your classroom walls.** Hang small mirrors as well as full-length ones. For infants, mirrors should lie horizontal at floor level. For bigger children, mirrors should be upright.

Does the Child Hear the Language of His Community and the Language of His Family?

In early childhood classrooms and family child care homes, children need intentional opportunities to hear and speak English. They also need support for their home language. The rules for language use should be explicit and straightforward. Make it obvious which language you want used when. For example, say, "Now we are speaking English," or, "Now we are speaking Spanish." Honor and respect both languages—but don't mix them.

It's important to understand the distinction between children's and adults' language mixing. Young children mix languages as part of their learning. Mixing is a developmentally appropriate and normal part of the language-learning process. But adults in the early childhood classroom are in a formal teaching role. Their job is to move children from social language to academic language. They have a responsibility to be careful in their language use.

Learning a language is similar to learning how to play a musical instrument. Let's imagine you are learning to play both the violin and the flute. Both instruments require you to know the same basic principles of music. But you must also learn a special set of knowledge and methods for each instrument. And you can't play the violin and the flute at the same time.

Here are some specific ideas to help you make sure your dual-language-learning students hear, learn, and honor both of their languages:

- **Greet children in their home language when they enter the room.** Use the correct pronunciation for their names.

- **Be explicit about the languages you hear or speak.** For example, say, "Today, we are saying 'good morning' in Spanish. We say, 'buenos días.'" In response to a child who names an apple in Spanish, you might say, "Ramón, you said it in Spanish. You are right, this is *una manzana*. And in English, it is an apple."

- **Select at least one day per week for singing songs in children's home languages.** Be explicit about it. Repeat the songs so all the children have time to learn them.

- **During small-group time, separate the children into same-language groups with a staff member or a volunteer who is literate in the language.** Have the adult read a book or tell a story and discuss it with the children.

- **Do not rely on home languages for giving directions.** For example, when a teacher makes a habit of saying, *"¡Siéntate!"* to get the children to sit down, the children do not hear Spanish in a positive way. They hear it as an expression of exasperation. This undermines the goal of honoring all the children's languages. The command would be just as understandable in English.

Does the Child Have the Right Materials to Learn in the Best Way?

I recently visited a classroom where the topic of study was animals of the northern forest. In the block area, the animal box contained only African animals. The children couldn't use the vocabulary of the northern forest with African animals.

It's not fair to the children to be casual about organizing your learning materials (Curtis and Carter 2003; Greenman 2005). It's also not a good idea to have too many materials. With too many materials, spaces become cluttered, and children can't see the relevance of materials to the topic of study. More is not better; it is confusing. For example, twenty-four different plastic vegetables and fruits lumped together in the dramatic play sink are too numerous to process.

Young children learn through hands-on experiences. The materials teachers offer them should match the overall theme or topic of study. This is particularly important for dual-language learners. Dual-language learners have a challenging job. They must make sense of many new words for objects and behaviors in their second language. They need carefully selected materials to focus their learning. Here are some tips for selecting and culling materials in your classroom:

- **Select materials and books that are most relevant to your current topic of study.** Leave out just a few favorites from the previous theme or topic.

- **Tour your room and ask yourself two questions for each item that's accessible to children:** How does it relate to our main topic of study? What do I want the children to learn from this item? If you do not have a quick answer, the item is not relevant enough. Put it away in storage and use it later.

- **Ruthlessly declutter your room walls.** This is not a matter of aesthetics; it is a matter of educational focus.

- **Do not use CDs for singing with the children.** CDs are usually too fast, and English-language learners cannot keep up. They end up doing the motions, but giving up on the words.

Does the Child Feel Calm, Not Overstimulated?

Children in group situations experience increasing stress as the day goes on (Gunnar et al. 2010). And because learning two languages is more work than learning one language, dual-language learners experience even more stress. To minimize this stress, plan your schedule and arrange your environment with calmness in mind. Here are some suggestions:

- **Examine your classroom every week and weed out everything that's not essential for your teaching that week.**

Classrooms can be visually overstimulating when every nook and cranny is crammed with stuff and the walls are crowded with posters, signs, labels, artwork, and so on. Your walls should display only what is essential for learning. The same goes for other materials in your room.

- **Evaluate your schedule carefully and count the transitions.** Transitions can be difficult and stressful for young children. The average early childhood classroom has nineteen to twenty transitions—even during a half-day session. Think about how you might eliminate some transitions from your day. You may need to experiment for several days until you hit upon the right daily rhythm for your class.

- **Keep consistent classroom routines.** Consistency enables children to recognize and predict what is happening and what will happen. It prevents distraction and confusion. It frees children to concentrate on learning.

- **Alternate activities that require a lot of language with activities that do not.** For example, don't read a book and then sing songs immediately afterward. After you read a book, concentrate on the language of the book and have a conversation about the story. Sing songs at a different time, such as at the end of a large-muscle activity.

- **Design a quiet place in your classroom.** When children need a break, they can go to the quiet place and look at books or play quietly on their own with puzzles or stuffed animals.

- **Turn off the CD player.** Dual-language learners must distinguish between different sounds and meanings all day long. Music and singing as a backdrop to other activities stress children's senses and reduce learning opportunities. In homes where the TV is on all the time, parents and children interact more than 20 percent less than in homes without background TV (Pearson Zurer 2008). A similar effect happens in classrooms with constant background music. The space fills with sounds instead of intentionally produced words. Reserve music for strategic use, such as playing soft, soothing music at naptime.

Planning an Effective Curriculum for Dual-Language Learners

A colleague e-mailed me the following joke: A little girl had just finished her first week of school. "I'm just wasting my time," she said to her mother. "I can't read, I can't write, and they won't let me talk!"

I chuckled. A joke hits the mark when we recognize the truth it contains. It's all too true that young children don't get enough practice talking—even though talking is the foundation for literacy (Copple and Bredekamp 2009).

Educators who teach dual-language learners must plan their curriculum carefully. The curriculum should include all the components you usually have for English speakers. In addition, you should pay extra attention to how you will use oral language.

Integrating the Curriculum with Themes and Projects

Themes and projects are valuable teaching strategies for focusing an early childhood curriculum. Children benefit from the structure that themes and projects provide over three or more weeks. Themes and projects integrate the curriculum, which allows children to build knowledge in an orderly way over a sustained period. Themes and projects give children time and opportunities to explore and practice. They also provide the space for adults to repeat and expand on some activities.

Themes and projects offer several benefits that are especially important for dual-language learners:

- Children learn more words as the topic expands.

- Repetition helps cement concepts and skills.

- Different approaches to the same topic capture children's attention.

- Common work promotes cooperation.

- Continuity aids learning.

Class projects are a learning approach in which children study a particular topic in depth (Helm and Katz 2011). The teacher chooses the topic or gathers ideas by observing children's interests. Once the teacher and students establish a general topic to study, they ask, "What do we want to find out?" They develop vocabulary and activities together, starting with what the children know and adding new words, concepts, and investigations as they ask questions about the topic.

For example, the children and staff may want to find out about trains. Staff members serve as resource providers and facilitators of exploration. With their help, the young investigators research trains in books or on the Internet. They take field trips and talk to experts (knowledgeable adults or older children). Children explore ideas about trains, ask questions, and find answers at their own pace through talking, manipulating, writing, drawing, construction, movement, and dramatic play. They encounter many opportunities for social play and problem solving. Staff members observe the children at work, take pictures, record dialogue, and take notes on the children's behavior. At the end of the train project, families come to view the children's work and celebrate the community of learners.

Themes are a learning approach similar to projects but more teacher directed. The teacher chooses a topic, researches the information, provides all the materials, and proposes all the activities. The success of a theme depends on the children's interest and their familiarity with the ideas. A theme is most effective when the topic is relevant to the children's lives. For example, children living in a small town might not be familiar with skyscrapers, so a skyscraper theme is risky. But they would certainly understand the concepts of houses and small apartment buildings. A theme about dwellings would be more effective.

Building Vocabulary

A thematic or project-based curriculum is an excellent way to develop vocabulary and expand children's understanding of their world. Sustain each project or theme for at least three weeks. Sustained study gives children more opportunities to hear and practice new words and concepts.

The diagram on the next page shows the vocabulary learned and explored by a classroom engaged in a theme about bears. The diagram shows how the vocabulary words fall into eight categories.

All these words provide rich opportunities for play and conversation. They also offer helpful guidance for activities and materials, such as books to read, new props in the dramatic play areas, science experiments, art and sensory explorations, and songs and fingerplays for circle time.

Practicing Oral Language

When conversation revolves around a theme or project, it is much more fun and meaningful for teachers and children. The speakers connect intellectually on a common study topic. This moves children from using only social language to using the academic language they need to succeed in school. During transitions, free play, and mealtimes, a theme or project expands the repertoire of conversation beyond simple chitchat. It also provides built-in conversation starters for adults and children who aren't naturally talkative. For example, I was witness to the dialogue on the next page during breakfast in an early childhood classroom:

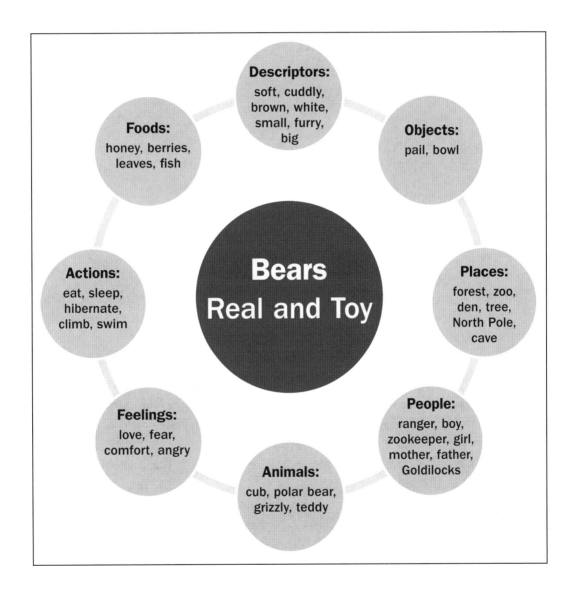

TEACHER: Remember what the theme for our class is?

CHILD 1: Bears!

TEACHER: What did we learn about bears?

CHILD 1: They . . . big! (*Extends arms to show large size.*)

CHILD 2: Berries!

TEACHER: Yes, bears can be very big, and they live in the forest, and true, they eat berries. Just like we are having today. Blueberries. (*Shows the blueberries in her bowl.*)

CHILD 3: Teddy bear?

TEACHER: You are thinking about cuddly teddy bears. Yours is pink.

CHILD 3: In my cubby.

TEACHER: Yes, your teddy bear is in your cubby. Teddy bears are not real bears; they are toys. Real bears, like the one in the video, are big. They don't fit in the cubby.

CHILDREN 1, 2, AND 3, *giggling*: Nooo! Too big!

The conversation continued for several more minutes. The three children at the table, all dual-language learners, had beginning English skills. The teacher facilitated the conversation, expanding it from the one-, two-, or three-word sentences they offered. All the while, she was also attending to the caretaking tasks of serving food and milk and wiping spills.

Planning a Language-Rich Curriculum

Dual-language learners need support from adults to learn new words, both in their home language and in English. They also need to initiate activities on their own. Ideally, your curriculum should include a balance of adult-directed and child-directed activities. You'll find examples of both in the following chart.

A language-rich curriculum connects vocabulary (words) and ideas (concepts) with the child's world and experiences outside school. The following scene from Ms. Martin's preschool classroom, where two-thirds of the children are dual-language learners who will move on to kindergarten next year, shows a language-rich curriculum at work.

Adult-Directed Activities	Child-Directed Activities
Facilitating discussions	Exploring sensory and manipulative materials
Facilitating play	Playing with other children
Asking questions	Asking questions
Charting ideas	Scribbling
Writing	Drawing
Reading	Building
Demonstrating	Dictating ideas to adults
Teaching early literacy skills (vocabulary, conversation, concepts of print, alphabet, and phonological awareness)	Pretending in dramatic play
	Looking at books independently

It is April in Minnesota, and everyone is ready for spring. Ms. Martin has chosen spring as the topic for her class project. She will explore this topic with the children for the next six weeks.

In Minnesota, after the long snowy season, the children see many spring signs in the trees, on the grass, in the clothes people wear, in the birds that fly around, in the gardens people plant, and in the daily conversations people have. The stores are selling bicycles, swimming suits, flowers, seeds, and sun hats. A lot is happening! Spring is relevant to children's everyday lives in this part of the world.

Ms. Martin starts the class project with a K-W-L exercise. She asks, "What do we *know* about spring? What do we *want to learn* about spring?" As the children explore the topic, they will assess what they have learned about spring.

In the K-W-L exercise, Ms. Martin finds that the children *know* about spring in a general sense. They know about snow melting, and grass getting green, and trees budding. They really *want to learn* how these things happen. The children express an interest in gardening. Designing a garden becomes the class project.

Ms. Martin finds books at the library and short videos on the Internet that explain the hows and whys of spring changes in nature. She invites a parent who is a gardener to help the children think about what they could plant. They decide that since they do not have an outdoor garden space, they will garden with pots in the classroom.

Ms. Martin fills each school day with new and interesting opportunities to learn words and concepts relating to spring. She writes lists of the children's questions and accounts of their discoveries. Ms. Martin and the children review these lists together each day at circle time. They chart the new words and ideas they learn. They repeat and practice these words and ideas through spring-related large-group activities, small-group activities, dramatic play, science experiments, sensory table work, talking, reading, and writing. The project lasts for six weeks. This sustained study gives children enough repetition to practice and master the language they're learning.

When I visit during the fourth week, I observe the children discussing the designs of their gardens, planting real and pretend seeds, and selling and buying garden tools in their play store. They are not just busy; rather, they are actively using words to talk, negotiate, and solve problems.

Reflection Questions

1. Look at your classroom through the eyes of a child who is learning two languages. For each of these children, how would you answer the five questions on page 88?

2. Think about your curriculum. Is it integrated to provide enough repetition of experiences so dual-language learners can learn information in multiple ways?

3. Pick one child to observe over a period of five days. Notice how the child uses the language of your theme or project. Write down the words and sentences you hear the child say. If you hear her use fewer than six topic-related words, make a plan to increase the language richness of your curriculum the following week.

Chapter 7

Techniques for Teaching English in the Multilingual Classroom

L et's look at two scenarios that might take place in a multilingual
preschool classroom. The children in the classroom are four- and five-
year-olds on their way to kindergarten. Mr. Ben is their teacher. The current topic of study is transportation. It is the middle of November.

Scenario 1: At the end of circle time, Mr. Ben asks the children to pick
a learning center. Carlitos and Mohamed both choose the block center.
It includes not only blocks but also small cars and trucks and a street
rug. Carlitos speaks Spanish at home, and Mohamed speaks Arabic. They
are learning English at school. Carlitos and Mohamed play together
for about fifteen minutes. They construct small buildings and bridges.
They guide their cars and trucks along the roads, avoiding obstacles.
They smile at each other and make engine sounds: *vroom, vroom, vroom!*
When one boy wants the vehicle that the other one has, he points to it.
The boys smile and exchange vehicles. They continue playing together:
vroom, vroom, vroom! Their cooperation is perfect and their social skills
are lovely, but they have no common language besides engine sounds.

Mr. Ben comments that Carlitos and Mohamed play so well together, they do not need him.

Scenario 2: At the end of circle time, Mr. Greg reminds the children of the words they have been studying this week: *fast, slow, truck, car, gas station, bridge,* and *road.* He demonstrates the words with gestures, pictures, and objects. He asks the children to say the words after him. The children eagerly repeat. Then Mr. Greg explains the options available in each learning center and asks the children to pick a center. He has posted the week's vocabulary words prominently on the wall as a reminder for the various adults who assist in the classroom.

Juan and Ali pick the center with blocks, vehicles, and a street rug. Juan speaks Spanish at home, and Ali speaks Arabic. They are learning English at school. Before dismissing them to the rug, Mr. Greg says, "You are going to the block center. You will play with the trucks and the cars. Some will go slow and some will go fast, like in our story." Juan and Ali play together for about fifteen minutes. They make small buildings and bridges. They guide their cars and trucks along the roads, avoiding obstacles. They smile at each other and make engine sounds: *vroom, vroom, vroom!* When one boy wants the vehicle that the other one has, he points to it. The boys smile and exchange vehicles. They continue playing together: *vroom, vroom, vroom!*

Ms. Mary, the teaching assistant, is circulating around the room. She notices Juan and Ali's play. She stops and watches them for fifteen seconds. As the children begin another exchange, she says, "Juan, you want the dump truck. Can you say, 'dump truck'?" Juan looks at Ali and says, "I dump truck." Ms. Mary smiles and repeats, "I want the dump truck. Juan, you are learning to use your words in English!" Ali gives the dump truck to Juan. Ms. Mary points at and names four of the vehicles the boys have placed on the street rug: "These are a dump truck, a blue truck, a tractor, and a car." She then leaves to attend to another group of children. When Ali wants the dump truck back, he taps Juan on the shoulder and says, "Dump truck, okay?" As they continue their play, they mix the engine sounds with the names of the vehicles. Their cooperation is perfect. Their social skills are lovely. English is emerging as their common language.

How are these scenarios similar? In both, it is the middle of November—about ten weeks into the school year. The children speak the same home languages and play with the same toys for the same length of time. How are these scenarios different? Only the second scenario contains intentional language teaching. In scenario 2 it's easy to imagine the progress Juan and Ali will make in learning English. In scenario 1 it's equally easy to picture the learning opportunities Carlitos and Mohamed will miss if the lack of intentional language teaching continues all year.

The Hard Work of Language Learning

Children who are learning two languages have to work very hard (Herrell 2000). They have to learn the languages and the ideas at the same time. Teachers can help these children learn efficiently by setting them up for success.

For example, it's easier to learn language and concepts within a familiar context. For any topic of study in your classroom, discover what the children already know. If your school is in a big city and you're planning to study forest animals, you might discover that the children know nothing about forest animals. In this case, you should start with animals they know that live in the city, and then introduce the idea that other animals live in different places, like the forest.

Remember that dual-language learners have to think extra hard to produce their new language. When asked a question, a dual-language learner has to decipher the question, formulate an answer, and figure out how to say that answer in the new language. In a large group, the pressure to answer quickly causes anxiety.

It's important to remove unnecessary obstacles for dual-language learners, but don't be afraid to provide intellectually engaging activities. Dual-language learners sometimes receive an oversimplified curriculum that stresses only the listing of words. Some educators worry that dual-language learners cannot answer open-ended questions, so they ask only yes-or-no questions. They do not help the children move to the next step. Avoid oversimplification. In a preschool classroom, for example, balance cutting-and-pasting activities with language-rich activities. In a primary-grade classroom, group children by ability to talk about a story they just heard and summarize what they liked best about it. Children with beginning English skills will make shorter sentences and make simpler comments. But they will also have more chances to talk if they are with other beginners. They need to practice, so this is better than being in a mixed group with proficient speakers who may take over the discussion.

Keep in mind each child's stage of second-language development. (See pages 51–54 for information about the stages of second-language development.) For example, if the child is at the nonverbal communication stage, you might ask a closed-ended question and have the child point. You might say, "Can you tell me where the cat is?" If the child points correctly to the cat in the tree, you know he understands the question, so his receptive language is accurate. If the child is at the telegraphic stage, you might try an open-ended question that requires a simple answer. For example, you might say, "Why did the cat climb the tree?" If the child says, "He scare," then we know the child understands the plot. If the child is at the productive stage, you can have a more extensive conversation. It is a good idea to put children in small groups of similar ability and to allow ample response time. Your goal is to help dual-language learners feel successful so they can progress with confidence.

In this chapter, you will find specific techniques that make it easier for dual-language learners to understand and practice English. I will focus on eight techniques that will give you the most return for your efforts:

1. small groups

2. modeled talk

3. scripted dramatic play

4. culture studies

5. peer tutoring

6. preview-view-review

7. dictation

8. total physical response

I will also explain techniques for teaching higher-order thinking skills and for reading in English to dual-language learners.

Small Groups

Learning to speak a language is a social process as well as a cognitive one. You can foster the social aspect of language learning by creating small groups. In a small-group setting, children feel more connected to one another, and friendships can grow. There are two ways to approach small-group time. Each has unique benefits.

- **Small groups of children with similar language abilities.**
  This approach works well when you want the children to practice

their speaking. The adult who facilitates the group can follow the pace of the children and make sure everyone has a turn.

- **Small groups of children with a mix of language abilities.** The advantage of this approach is that the English-proficient children can model English for the beginners. The adult who facilitates this group must watch the pace and slow it down if it gets too quick for the beginners.

Modeled Talk

Modeled talk is giving children the words they need when you join them in play or in conversation. For example, Anita and Sara are playing in the beauty shop. Anita speaks Spanish, while Sara speaks Russian. Anita is putting nail polish on Sara's fingers. They are obviously familiar with nail polish and beauty parlors, but they are playing silently. The girls do not know enough common words to converse. The teacher joins in.

TEACHER: Anita, I see you are putting nail polish on Sara's fingernails.
(*Anita and Sara look up and smile.*)

TEACHER: It is pink.

ANITA: Pink.

TEACHER: You like pink.

SARA: Like pink.

ANITA (*TO SARA*): More pink?

Sara and Anita have good receptive language. They understand what the teacher is saying. But they do not yet have the productive language they need to converse. Without the teacher's help, they would continue to play silently and would miss out on the opportunity to learn and practice English.

The teacher stays with Sara and Anita for another few minutes. The conversation continues. Anita and Sara use more words and are clearly enjoying their interaction.

Scripted Dramatic Play

With scripted dramatic play, the teacher initiates the play rather than only providing materials. This technique works best when the dramatic play you have set up is well integrated into your current theme and you have chosen key vocabulary to teach. Dual-language learners may not know many words in their new language, but they are likely to have a lot of background knowledge. First assess their background knowledge by observing their play. Then introduce and help them learn English vocabulary words that build on their knowledge. For example, if you have set up a grocery store, the props illustrate the key vocabulary words. These words are the same as those you read to the class in books.

Mr. Ben has targeted the words that he wants the children to learn: *supermarket, groceries, buy, sell, dollars, breads, farm, city, grocery store, vegetables, meat, fish, eggs, fruits, kitchen, cans, cook, bake,* and *spices.* These words are in the book he is reading this week. He wants the children to understand and use these words actively. Mr. Ben has posted the words on the classroom wall as a reminder. He has also modeled how to use the words in context, with the help of his assistant, Ms. Mary:

MR. BEN: Ms. Mary, I am in your grocery store, and I want to buy food for my dinner.

MS. MARY: Okay, Mr. Ben, what do you want to buy?

MR. BEN: I want meat and vegetables for soup.

MS. MARY: Here you go, Mr. Ben, vegetables and meat for your soup. It is ten dollars, please.

As the children play in the grocery store, Mr. Ben intentionally mentions the words. When he sees Sonia handing the bread to Li silently, he says: "Sonia, you sell the bread to Li. Li, you buy the bread." With this technique, the children learn vocabulary as they play.

Culture Studies

Why not take direct advantage of the multicultural richness in your group of children, families, and educators? Everyone has a cultural story to tell.

Hang a large map of the world on your classroom wall. Place a pin at your current location. For all the children and staff members, stretch a piece of yarn from the pin to wherever they or their family came from. Include ancestors, if necessary. For example, a child in Minneapolis, Minnesota, might say, "I was born in Minneapolis, but my grandma was born in Guadalajara, Mexico." On the map, the yarn for that child would stretch from a pin at Minneapolis to a pin at Guadalajara.

The map can serve as a guide to discussions about housing, food, games, alphabets, transportation, nature, history, geography—and of course language—in different places. Whenever you introduce a new topic of study, the map will provide a built-in reminder for expansion.

For example, when you begin a unit of study on transportation, think about the transportation people use where you live now. Then discuss what the children and families know about transportation in their home countries. What are the vehicles? What are the vehicles called in the families' home languages? What is the geography (mountain roads, freeways, walking paths, rivers, and so on)? Examine the similarities and differences between here and there.

Is this technique relevant for babies and toddlers? Yes, because when you work with a child, you work with the child's family, too. Family members drop off and pick up their children. When they do so, they can look at the map and talk about it with their children, with other parents, and with teachers. They'll find commonalities and will share in the joy of their diverse community of learners.

Peer Tutoring

Peer tutoring is possible in schools that serve a wide range of ages from birth to eight years old. In these schools, first graders could play with three-year-olds, second graders could play with kindergartners, and so on. Older children automatically adapt their tone, pace, and vocabulary when they speak with younger children. In a diverse urban school I frequently visit, they have designated Friday afternoon for peer tutoring. Dual-language learners and monolingual English speakers are paired randomly, as the numbers do not match exactly. The older students prepare for their session by practicing the reading of a book during the week. On Friday, they read the book in English to a younger child, talk about the story, and draw a picture together in their journals. This activity takes thirty minutes, and it is a lovely end to the week. It is also a practical way to promote language skills as a benefit for all. The younger children look up to the older children, and the older children feel they are making a valuable contribution, which they are. Peer tutoring takes careful coordination, but it can be very rewarding for both older and younger children.

Preview-View-Review

This technique works well to increase children's comprehension when you're reading a book to them or presenting a lesson on any topic. When you use this strategy, children get scaffolding both before and after straining to understand the book or presentation in English. The technique has three parts:

1. Preview: Preview the book or lesson in the home language. Give the title of the book and a brief summary of the plot, or briefly summarize the lesson.

2. View: Read the book or present the lesson in English.

3. Review: Discuss the book or lesson in the home language.

Dictation

Dictation is an activity in which the children dictate their ideas to the teacher, who writes down the ideas. You can try group dictation or individual dictation.

Group Dictation

After reading a story, the teacher asks the children what they remember about it. First the teacher models: "I remember there was a bear in the story." Then the teacher writes those words on the board. As the children say what they remember, the teacher records their words, phrases, and sentences. In a large group, this technique gives dual-language learners the chance to contribute with one or two words even if they do not have full productive language.

Individual Dictation

Here's how individual dictation works in a multilingual classroom: The teacher asks the children, one by one, to describe the pictures they've painted. The responses play out in three different ways, depending on the children's and the teacher's language skills:

- When a child dictates in English, the teacher writes whatever the child says in English.

- When a child dictates in a home language the teacher knows, the teacher writes the child's words in the home language. The teacher says, "You said it in [language]. Let's write what you said." Then the teacher reads the dictation aloud and says, "Let's say it in English now. Then you will have your story in two languages."

- When a child dictates in a home language the teacher doesn't know, the teacher says, "You said it in [language], but I cannot write [language]. I can write English. Can you tell me in English?" Then the teacher writes what the child says in English. If the child does not respond, the teacher says, "I know you want to write in [language]. Let's put a note on your drawing, and your family can help you at home tonight."

Total Physical Response

Total physical response is a sequence of actions that includes demonstration by the teacher, repetition by the children, and then a game of verbal commands. This technique is well suited to very young children, because young children learn by moving.

First you introduce the concepts and commands you want to use in your game, acting them out as you say them. The children repeat your words and actions. Then you begin the game, giving verbal commands to perform physical actions. The game works best when the commands include names of students and teachers, body parts, colors, movement verbs, directions, numbers, shapes, classroom procedures, and vocabulary that you can illustrate with pictures or real objects. For example:

- Play the game Simon Says, using commands like *touch your nose*, *touch your arm*, *touch the square*, or *touch the rectangle*. Or play the game with procedural commands, such as *sit down*, *stand up*, *go to the snack table*, *pick up your pencils*, or *open your book*.

- Say, "When you see the color red, stand up. When you see the color blue, sit down."

- Say, "When you see the bear, point to it." Or, "Point to the bear. Point to the bed. Point to the bowl."

- Display a set of pictures related to a book you've read, such as *Goldilocks and the Three Bears*, either out of order or with a few pictures from a different story. Say, "Put the pictures in order." Or, "Separate the Goldilocks pictures from the Rapunzel pictures."

One by one, give the children chances to lead the game—first without words, then with words. The children can play in pairs and in small groups. Simon Says is hard work for dual-language learners, if they do not know the vocabulary well. But it is also fun and active. Therefore it is a good teaching technique that is developmentally appropriate. The object is to find strategies that work well to maximize the learning.

Teaching Higher-Order Thinking Skills to Dual-Language Learners

Concept development, language skills, and mental ability go hand in hand (Burns, Griffin, and Snow 1999; Vukelich, Christie, and Enz 2002). The more words and ideas children have in their heads, the more they can think about. The more ideas children can articulate in words, pictures, and gestures, the better they can handle new ideas. As children grapple with new ideas, their brains build connections that expand their cognitive potential. This, in turn, permits children to develop the higher-order thinking skills they need to succeed in school:

- analyzing
- creating
- comparing
- classifying
- inferring
- integrating knowledge

How can teachers help children climb this mountain? They can use discussions and activities to encourage analysis and problem solving. Here's an example:

Tom is five years old. He is learning English as his second language. His receptive vocabulary is stronger than his productive vocabulary. He usually speaks one- and two-word sentences.

Tom has been building a ramp for cars in the block area. As he sends the cars down the ramp, they fall over the side. He is getting frustrated. His teacher points to the ramp and says sympathetically, "The cars are falling over the side." Tom looks up and nods.

"You want the cars to stay on the ramp," says the teacher. She guides one car all the way down the ramp. Tom nods again.

"What would help?" asks the teacher. Tom forms railings with his hands on the sides of the ramp. The teacher says, "Yes, railings would help—like the ones on the slide outside." Tom and the teacher stare silently at the ramp for a few seconds.

"Do you think tape would help?" asks the teacher. She walks over to the art shelf, picks up a roll of masking tape, and hands it to Tom. He then goes to the shelf himself and grabs strips of construction paper. He returns and shows them to the teacher, saying, "Tape."

She says, "Tom, you are going to tape this paper to the ramp to make railings. Good idea!"

As Tom starts taping the paper to the ramp, the teacher calls Ricky over to help. Tom and Ricky work together to finish the railings. Then they send a car down the ramp. It stays on!

Tom calls out, "Teacher, teacher, look, look, tape good!"

The teacher comes over and says, "Tom, the railings work! The cars are not falling anymore. You solved the problem." She claps, and Tom beams.

Tom observes a problem. The teacher does not give him the solution, but rather gives him opportunities to generate ideas and try them out. Because Tom is a dual-language learner, the teacher uses simple sentences, gestures, and objects to aid comprehension. She links to other knowledge Tom has, like the fact that the playground slide has sides to keep people from falling off. This real-world connection helps Tom integrate his learning. He eventually solves his engineering problem. He does it with words, analysis, and experimentation.

Tom's teacher understands the ultimate goal of her classroom materials, curriculum, and teaching. The block center is not just for learning about buildings and vehicles. It's for expanding minds. "The concept development dimension is not just about the development of a specific concept (e.g., seasons, subtraction) but about teachers' use of strategies to encourage understanding and thinking skills" (Pianta, LaParo, and Hamre 2008, 62).

I have noticed that many teachers forget this principle when they work with dual-language learners. They try to simplify the curriculum, and it becomes a superficial introduction of individual concepts instead of a means of developing academic language and higher-order thinking skills. For example, a dramatic play center might consist of a flower shop set up with various bouquets of silk flowers and a cash register. Once the children pretend to sell and buy flowers a few times, they do not know what else to do. Their play peters out, and so does their learning.

Here are some tips for teaching higher-order thinking skills to dual-language learners:

- Plan activities that last three to six weeks so children have time to experiment.

- Add more props each week to make the exploring more complex.

- Engage directly with the children so you can ask questions or help them solve problems.

- Connect children with each other so they can work together.

- Listen to what they say, even when they are at the telegraphic or two-word stage.

- Use simple sentences, gestures, and objects to aid comprehension.

- Celebrate their discoveries by using specific words to describe what they did.

Reading in English to Dual-Language Learners

Read a variety of books to give the children a well-rounded literary experience. Include books with predictable text, books with good stories, and informational books.

- **Read books with predictable text.** Many experts recommend this type of book for dual-language learners, because the repetition of the text in a recurring phrase and the repetition of the concepts make it easier to learn the vocabulary. Books with predictable text have enjoyable rhythm. Children can easily anticipate the ends of sentences and chime in. Repetitive books are wonderful for teaching phonological awareness and counting, but they are often too simple to challenge children's thinking skills.

- **Read books with good stories.** We want dual-language learners to enjoy and understand good stories, because we want to challenge their thinking with an interesting plot. A good story has an interesting plot, with a clear beginning, middle, and end. The narrative helps children understand cause and effect, discover relationships among characters and events, and solve problems. Stories about families are the most relevant to children's daily experiences. Choose short stories about human families with realistic illustrations or photographs that aid in the comprehension. Books with poetic language and abstract illustrations are confusing for children who have limited vocabulary in English. They cannot make sense of the meaning without visual aids.

- **Read informational books.** Informational books show children that they can learn from books as well as enjoy them. Immigrant parents who are not highly educated tend to view books as informational tools rather than entertainment. These parents are more apt to talk with their children about what an informational book says.

The books you choose should be related to your current topic of study. Be aware that most storybooks will take three to five minutes when read straight through. Dialogic reading adds another five to ten minutes to the reading session. (See the next section for more information on dialogic reading.) Timing is particularly important for dual-language learners because their attention span is shortened by the challenge of paying attention to a new language. If the reading is beyond their capacity to concentrate, they will be lost and won't learn much.

When choosing the degree of difficulty, consider not only the children's English comprehension but also their developmental level. The content should be at or slightly above their developmental level. In order to stimulate thinking, some books should be easy to grasp while others are more challenging—but not so challenging that they are overwhelming.

Here are some tips you can use to select the books and prepare for reading. Not all the elements have to be present in every book, but most should be.

- **Choose a book carefully.** Does it tell a good story? Does it use repetition of words and ideas? Does it take five minutes or less to read aloud? Does it have an enjoyable, predictable rhythm? Does it have a concrete ending? Are the illustrations or photographs realistic?

- **Read the book yourself before reading it to the children.** This will help you refine your expression and find actions and props you can use to aid children's comprehension.

- **Summarize the book.** Write three to six main ideas from the book that you want the children to understand and enjoy. Use simple sentences with key words from the story.

- **Teach vocabulary.** Find and write six to ten vocabulary words to teach from this book.

Once you have selected a book and know it well, it's time to read. The following read-aloud practices are effective ways to read in English with dual-language learners:

- **Dialogic reading:** Dialogic reading is the technique of reading and discussing a book at the same time. While reading, the adult pauses to point at pictures and draw attention to important items, ask questions, and answer children's questions. This technique helps children engage more in the reading and learn more from it. The slow pace helps the dual-language learners listen to the words, and the pointing gives them the visual cues to understand the story or the information. If they are not yet fluent, they may not ask questions, but they may make one-word comments such as, "bear," "happy," "big!" The reader should acknowledge these comments, as they show that the children are interested and actively participating in the reading.

- **Repeated read-aloud:** Repeated read-aloud is the technique of reading one featured book several days in a row. The repetition helps children understand the story well. With solid understanding, the children can participate more in discussions and analyze the characters and plot. They learn more vocabulary when they have more opportunities to hear and use the words (Schickedanz 2008). Repeated read-aloud is especially helpful for dual-language learners because it gives them the opportunity to hear the words many times. So if they get only some of the language on the first day, they will get more on the other days. It is the same process as when we watch a movie more than once. Each time we notice something we missed the previous time. Think of it as cumulative learning. Read the book straight through on the first day, pointing to the illustrations as you go or using appropriate props. Then read and stop for comments and questions on each of the following days. When I observe classrooms that use this technique, I notice full participation from the third day on with children anticipating the next page and the next event. The goal of comprehension is met! That is an important accomplishment for the students and the teacher that cannot be achieved by reading a different book every day.

Here are some tips for reading aloud in English to dual-language learners.

- **Do repeated readings (three to five per week) in one large group or two half groups.** Read with expression. Gestures and facial expressions help dual-language learners understand the text better. Show excitement when the character is excited or sadness when the character is sad. Summarize the story after each reading in short sentences with the same words as in the book. For example, after reading *The Very Hungry Caterpillar*, you might say, "The caterpillar becomes a butterfly. A beautiful butterfly." This helps the children hear the key vocabulary. Keep your summary short to avoid overwhelming the children. Fewer but clearer words are better.

- **Teach oral language skills.** Plan three activities related to the story to do at other times of the day so children can practice conversation. Reading a children's book takes about five to ten minutes. If this is the only exposure that children have to the vocabulary, it is not enough time to learn. Dual-language learners need more occasions to use the words they are learning. If you are reading *Goldilocks and the Three Bears*, you have many options for repeating the words from the story in other situations. Using the rule of three suggested above, you might consider: (1) talking at the snack table about Goldilocks's adventures; (2) having bowls and other objects of different sizes in the math center; (3) playing alliteration games with words beginning with the Bb sound while waiting for the school bus: "*bear, big, bowl.*" I am sure you are coming up with even more ideas now. Imagine how much the children will enjoy these conversations on a topic they know, and how their confidence in using English will grow.

- **Involve families.** Choose one activity you will use for the school-home link. Write a note to parents—or a script for talking with them—that explains how to do the activity. Inviting parents to do the activity in their home language is a way to honor and support their language, as well as a way to engage parents and children together on a fun project. For example, you may give the parents the vocabulary for all the fruit that the hungry caterpillar eats, and ask them to look for real fruit at the supermarket, or pictures of fruit in the supermarket flyer, or taste these fruits at home.

- **Evaluate your reading.** How did it go? How did the children react? What did they learn? How did the parents react? You will certainly have some reading experiences that are better than others are, which is why I recommend you evaluate how each reading goes. Realizing what could have gone better allows you to make changes for the next time. Perhaps you picked a book that was too complicated and the children lost interest. Use the evaluation to continue your readings on a positive note.

You can use the following chart (pages 114–17) as a planning tool for reading English books aloud to the children.

Reading Plan

Book Title: The Little Red Hen   **Date:** 2/29/12

Does this book:	Notes:
☐ have a predictable text?	Yes, through repetition: "Not I, She said."
☐ tell a good story?	Yes
☐ convey information?	About making flour with wheat and making bread with flour. About feelings, and hard work.
☐ have an enjoyable rhythm?	Yes
☐ use repetition?	Yes, repetition, the children can chime in
☐ challenge or stimulate the children's thinking?	Yes, helping vs. not helping friends
☐ have an interesting plot?	Yes, don't know until the end what the little red hen will do
☐ have a concrete beginning, middle, and ending?	Yes
☐ depict experiences relevant to the children's daily lives?	Consequences when we don't help. How to make bread
☐ have realistic photographs and illustrations?	Illustrations: realistic animals, bread, stove

☐ relate to our current topic of study?	Breads of the world. We are learning about breads from the different countries the children's families come from. This story shows how to make bread. In addition, we are exploring the idea of friendship and helping each other in our classroom. We will reenact the story next week, with both themes. We will be making bread in the classroom with parent volunteers.
☐ take 5–10 minutes to read aloud?	Yes
☐ meet the children's comprehension levels?	Not on the first day. Will learn vocabulary each day. See below.
☐ meet the children's developmental levels?	Yes
Supporting Materials What actions and props can I use to aid the children's comprehension?	Point to realistic pictures in the book Show a real loaf of bread Show stove and oven in dramatic play Shake head and finger for "Not I" Excited face and nod head for "I will"
Summary What main ideas (3–6) from the book do I want the children to understand and enjoy?	1. The little red hen works hard and enjoys the fruit of her labor 2. How to make bread 3. How friends need to help each other so they can enjoy life together too

Vocabulary What vocabulary words (6–12) do I want to teach from this book?	Day 1: Hen, goose, bread (already know cat and dog) Day 2: Wheat, grow, flour Day 3: Cut, wheelbarrow, oven Day 4: Thresh, bake, loaf
Repeated Readings (3–5 per week) When will I read the book? Will I read it to one large group or two half groups?	I will read the book to the whole group in English on Monday, Wednesday, Thursday, and Friday. On Tuesday, our Spanish bilingual educator comes. She will read the book in Spanish to the Spanish-speaking children. They will discuss it with her in Spanish. This will help with comprehension the rest of the week in English.
Oral Language Skills What are 3 activities related to the story to be done at other times of the day so the children can practice conversation?	Talk about the steps for making bread at lunch. Talk about helping friends while waiting for the bus. Make bread in the dramatic play bakery. Have recipe books, with pictures. Write recipes and lists of ingredients.

Family Involvement	Ask parents to talk about the bread of their home country. If their culture does not have bread, talk about the alternative. If they have bread, make some, or buy some and share together.
What are 1–3 activities I will use for the school-home link?	Talk about sharing with and helping friends.
Evaluation	The children liked the story. By the third day, they chimed in with "not I" and "I will" with gusto. Some understood the true meaning when we reenacted on the last day, and the dogs, the cats, and the geese had to watch the hens eat and not them. So they decided to reenact again next week, with everybody helping and . . . eating together!
How did it go? How did the children react? What did they learn? How did the parents react?	They understood the steps for making bread. That's good preparation for baking for real next week.
	Four parents said their children were very curious about bread this week.

Note: A reproducible template of this chart is provided in the appendix.

It is, of course, important to read books in the home language also. I will address how to do that in the next chapter.

Reflection Questions

1. Review the list of techniques in this chapter. Are there any you are not using that you would like to try? Choose two and begin to use them. In order to give a new technique a fair try, you need to practice for two weeks. At the end of two weeks, evaluate your use of the technique. How is it going? Note how the children are learning.

2. Review the example on teaching higher-order thinking skills. Observe a child in your classroom. How is the child using language to solve problems? What could you do to enhance the child's learning?

Chapter 8

Techniques for Supporting the Home Language

When a teacher found out about the multilingual composition of her classroom, she was so worried about what to do that she had nightmares. In her dreams, nobody understood anyone else, and all the children were running around and screaming wildly. The teacher was under pressure from her director to get the children ready for English kindergarten. And she was anxious and unsure about how to support the children's home languages. Doing both seemed like an impossible task.

In chapter 7, we discussed how to teach English to young dual-language learners. Teachers also have a professional responsibility to support children in maintaining their home languages (Castro, Ayankoya, and Kasprzak 2011). But why is this important? And how can it be done?

Why Support Home Languages?

For dual-language learners, keeping up the home language is important for three key reasons. Home-language skills help children

- maintain their emotional and family connections
- maintain their cultural connections
- increase their mental ability

The home language is the language of emotions and family relationships. A baby hears the home language before birth. It is the first language the baby hears after birth. Parents use it to say "I love you," to sing lullabies, and to coax their baby to eat one more spoonful of mashed bananas. They also use the home language for correction when baby grows older and misbehaves. When the child becomes a teenager, home-language skills make parent-child discussions easier.

The home language is the language of the family's home culture. As time passes, the child can use this language with relatives and friends of the family. If grandparents live nearby, they can talk to the child about life in the home country. If they live far away, they can call the child on the telephone or use the Internet to chat or e-mail. Since culture involves shared memories and activities bound by language, home-language skills give the child a sense of belonging.

In short, language is about not just words but also how we use words to view and interact with the world. Families and cultures use words in unique ways. When children learn these words and patterns, they build bonds with their families and communities.

Finally, research shows that bilingualism is an asset. It makes the brain more nimble and increases mental ability. It can improve understanding of cultures and the similarities and differences among cultures. And it offers many economic advantages.

The scientific literature clearly supports home-language instruction (Espinosa 2010). But researchers do not provide clear recommendations on how to do it. In this chapter, I will give you a formula for supporting home languages in a variety of circumstances. What you do will depend on the human resources you have. You might have bilingual staff (a lead teacher, assistant teacher, or floating bilingual educator), family volunteers, or community volunteers. The ideas that follow are designed for the classroom and for the home-classroom connection. In the classroom, staff or volunteers will implement them. For the home-school connection, it will be the families' job to maintain the home language, with guidance from you.

Three Simple Rules

Regardless of your circumstances, you can do a good job of supporting home languages if you follow three simple rules:

- Provide continuity.
- Be predictable.
- Be explicit.

Provide Continuity

Provide continuity in the concepts, the vocabulary, and the activities you present so the children's learning is integrated. Coordinate your home-language books and activities with the current topic of study in your classroom. For example, if you are studying transportation in English, your vocabulary words might include *bus, taxi, driver, parking lot, gas station, gas, car wash, park, haul, drive, key, large, small, close,* and *far.* You should use the same vocabulary in the home-language activities. Such repetition helps children understand and learn the words in their home language and recognize the words in English. This dual mastery helps them have more fun and feel more competent.

Be Predictable

Make home-language learning a part of your daily or weekly routine. Include home-language activities in your schedule on a regular, predictable pattern. For example, if children know that they will sing a Spanish song every day at the end of circle time, then they learn to anticipate it. This anticipation is good for all the children, because it honors the language of the Spanish speakers, it gives their language an official place in the classroom, and all the children gain phonological awareness by singing songs in Spanish.

Be Explicit

Children can sense when people speak different languages. But letting children guess what's happening slows them down needlessly. Learners learn best when they know what they are learning. Be explicit about the languages you use in your classroom. For example, say, "Girls and boys, we are going to sing our next song in French. Remember, we sing in French every Tuesday. Martine and Olivier speak French at home, and we are learning to sing like them!" Or you might say, "In English, we say 'butterfly,' and in Somali, we say '*balanbaalis.*' The words sound different, don't they? But they say the same thing!"

Monolingual or Bilingual, You Can Do It

I find that monolingual teachers worry they cannot support the home languages of their students because they themselves speak only English. It is of course easier to support home languages when teachers are multilingual. But attitude is more valuable than skill in this case.

Monolingual English-Speaking Educators

Educators who are monolingual English speakers can support children's home languages in important ways, even though they can't speak the languages. Teachers demonstrate interest and respect when they learn about home languages and cultures. Teachers show affection and compassion when they use greetings and comfort words in home languages. Teachers show that they value their families' home-language literacy (oral and written) when they let children share ideas or items from home, or when teachers invite family members to tell stories or read books in the classroom. Teachers preserve the dignity of home languages when they consistently give children directions (sit down, wash hands, and so on) in English—with the help of gestures, smiles, and patience—rather than in home languages. They avoid sending the message that home languages are for humble purposes only.

Teachers promote home-language learning when they give children structured time and activities for home-language instruction. Teachers promote home-language learning when they use bilingual staff or volunteers who are trained and supported and who follow a lesson plan coordinated with the rest of the curriculum. And teachers promote home-language learning when they include a home-school link in all their lesson planning.

Bilingual Educators

Bilingual educators can support children's home languages in all the same ways as educators who are monolingual English speakers. And with their additional language skills, bilingual educators can offer extra support.

Bilingual educators support children's learning when they use the home language for comfort if children have separation anxiety and are sad. It is important to respond to children with sensitivity when they are distressed. When we do so, we address the emotional part of language.

Bilingual educators also support children's learning by teaching songs and games, reading books, facilitating small groups in home languages, and not mixing languages. When bilingual educators use home languages according to a carefully developed language plan, they help children increase vocabulary, concepts, oral language, and positive self-esteem and relationships. Home languages get stronger and become the foundation for learning English and developing early literacy skills.

Strategies for Home-Language Instruction

In the following sections, I offer five strategies for using a home language for classroom instruction:

1. reading in the home language

2. small-group time

3. circle-time songs and fingerplays

4. circle-time greetings

5. individual greetings

The strategies appear in order of intensity, from high intensity to low intensity. How you carry out these suggestions will depend on the human resources available to you. If you have permanent staff who are fully bilingual and can talk, read, and write in the home language, you should include home-language instruction in your daily schedule. If you have intermittent access to bilingual staff or volunteers, you may have to space your home-language activities differently.

Reading in the Home Language

You should use the same technique for reading in the home language as you use for reading in English. Take the same care in selecting books, preparing, and reading. See pages 110–118 for more information.

Small-Group Time

Home-language small-group time gives children opportunities to practice their home language and develop their higher-order thinking skills. During your scheduled small-group time, separate the children into language groups. Use the small-group time to read a book related to your current topic of study.

- **Approach 1: Three times per week.** If you have permanent bilingual staff, you have the lucky option of providing frequent and regular readings in the home languages. This method typically consists of three twenty- to thirty-minute sessions per week.

  ○ Session 1: Read the book you have been reading as a repeated read-aloud in English. (See page 112 for more information on repeated read-alouds.) Discuss the book in the home language.

  ○ Session 2: Reread the same book. Help the children summarize the book in the home language. Write down their ideas.

  ○ Session 3: Read a different book on the same topic with similar vocabulary. Discuss the book in the home language. Ask questions to help children compare the books. Write down their ideas.

- **Approach 2: One time per week.** If you have access to bilingual staff only one day per week, hold your home-language reading at the beginning of the week. That way, you can introduce the children to the week's main book and key vocabulary in their home language, and then continue in English throughout the rest of the week. A home-language foundation will make it easier for the children to continue the week's work in English.

Circle-Time Songs and Fingerplays

In each home language of your classroom, choose two songs or finger-plays related to your current topic of study. If you have a recording of a song or fingerplay, listen to it as an introduction only, to help you remember the words or the tune. Then turn off the recording and use your own voices. In order to participate fully, children need a slower pace than most recordings offer. I have observed many circle times with CDs. During these circle times, the pace went too quickly, and the children could not follow along, so they simply listened. Circle time became entertainment time instead of learning time.

Circle-Time Greetings

At the beginning of the day, many teachers hold a circle time to greet the entire group of children. This is a great way to build community among learners. Some groups sing a name song or a good-morning song. In some classrooms, the children turn to each other and say hello.

You can incorporate home languages into your circle-time greeting. Choose one day for each home language in your classroom. For example, you might choose Monday for English, Tuesday for Spanish, Wednesday for Somali, and so on. If you have more home languages than days of the week, use a two-week rotation of languages. Remember to be explicit about your language use. For example, you might say, "Yesterday was Monday, and we sang our good-morning song in English. Today is Tuesday, and we will sing our good-morning song in Vietnamese. That's the language that Ms. Van and Kim-Ly speak at home."

Individual Greetings

In some early childhood programs, families drop off their children. In others, the children arrive by bus. As the children arrive, individual greetings help them reconnect with their teachers and classmates. When educators use simple home-language greetings to welcome children, they help build warm relationships.

I once visited a classroom of four-year-olds in mid-February. In this classroom, the children had grown familiar with individual home-language greetings. They started to play jokes on the teacher, greeting her in a language different from their own. Ben, an English speaker, and

Mohamed, a Somali speaker, would walk in the door saying, *"¡Buenos días!"* and then giggle their way to the sign-in table. The children's playfulness showed their sophisticated understanding of language. They had learned a lot through their teacher's explicit home-language instruction.

Home-School Link

Children learn best when adults provide continuity between home and school. Continuity is especially important for dual-language learners, because families and teachers cannot promote both languages without each other's help.

With a strong early childhood curriculum, children encounter more ideas and do more activities than they might at home. For example, day and night are familiar concepts for children. They know that they sleep at night and wake in the morning. They know about the sun and moon and the different clothes they wear at night and during the day. In the early childhood classroom, children get a chance to expand their knowledge and skills as they explore the theme of day and night more deeply. They learn more vocabulary, they do art and science activities, and they read books that stimulate their intellect.

When educators engage families in the curriculum, they expand children's knowledge and skills even further. Engaging families gives children the opportunity to talk with their parents at home about the same topics they discussed at school with their teachers. It is a good way to reinforce information and increase learning—and a benefit to all children, of course. Dual-language learners get the extra benefit of strengthening their home language when they talk or read with their parents. A strong home-school connection also gives immigrant families a practical way to foster their children's home-language learning.

Informing Families about Topics of Study

Families in general usually don't know exactly what their children are learning in early childhood education programs. Immigrant families tend to feel even more disconnected. But from the research and from my own work, I know that immigrant families want their children to do well in school. If educators invite immigrant families to collaborate with them, the families are likely to respond favorably.

You can inform and engage families either orally or in writing. You might speak to a family through an interpreter during a home visit or during a brief meeting at school. Or you might connect with families in writing. Here are some guidelines for a biweekly letter to immigrant families.

- Type the letter in a standard typeface, such as Times New Roman, using a twelve-point font size and double-spaced lines.

- Use plain language, with no jargon. Aim for a reading level below fifth grade. You can have your letter translated or send it in English. Immigrants who don't read well can usually find someone to help them read and understand documents.

- Use a classic business-letter format.

- Start with a personal greeting.

- Give the title of the book you are reading for your main read-aloud, with a short description of the story. Add a picture of the book cover, if possible.

- List the key words you are teaching the children.

- Ask the families to do two activities with their children at home. Explain what the children will learn from these activities.

- End with a personal thank-you and a formal signature.

- Keep the length at one page.

On the next page you'll find a sample letter to immigrant families. The reading level of this letter is grade 4.2.

Dear Families:

Greetings to you! It is a pleasure to teach your children in my classroom every day.

For the next two weeks, we will be learning about night and day. This is part of our study of the world. We will talk about the sky and the earth and about the different things people do at night and during the day.

For the first week, we are reading the book *Goodnight Moon*. The author is Margaret Wise Brown. For the second week, we are reading the book *Who Likes the Sun?* The authors are Beatrice Schenk de Regniers and Leona Pierce.

At school, we will do many activities about day and night using art, science, and blocks. The children will also make pictures and write stories in their journals. The children are learning about day and night in English at school. It is important that they also learn these ideas in the language of your home.

I am teaching the children these words in English: *day, night, sun, star, moon, earth, light, dark, shine, sleep, dream,* and *shadow*. At home, please talk about the same words in your home language.

I also ask that you do two activities:

1. During the day, look for shadows on the sidewalk, on the wall, or on the sides of buildings.

2. During the night, take your child outside for two minutes. Look at the sky to see the stars or the moon.

When teachers and families work together, the children learn more and are better students. Thank you for being my partner!

Teacher Angèle

Combining English Teaching and Home-Language Support

In this section, I discuss a variety of ways to combine English instruction and home-language support, based on four different student and staff scenarios:

1. honoring and teaching home languages

2. honoring home languages

3. teaching infants and toddlers

4. teaching home languages to children in kindergarten through third grade

Teaching Home Languages

This approach is possible when you have bilingual educators or volunteers who are qualified to teach in the home language. They are fully literate in the home language, and they know how to do dialogic reading. For example, the families of the children in a classroom speak Spanish, Somali, Russian, and English at home. The classroom lead teacher and two assistants are bilingual in English/Spanish, English/Somali, and English/Russian. All are literate in English and the home language and can teach in the home language.

Talking, reading, and writing are in English during most of the day. Home-language instruction occurs in small groups at the same time every day, following the same thematic curriculum as the English instruction. All the classroom materials and books are in English, Spanish, Somali, and Russian. To honor all the home languages, all the children participate in large-group activities that include greetings, songs, and visitors from each language.

The teachers encourage the children's families to use their home language at home. Families receive ideas and resources related to the classroom curriculum.

Here are some classroom suggestions you can use with this approach:

- Conduct story time in English, with repeated read-alouds. Home-language staff or volunteers use the preview-view-review technique.

- Conduct large-group time in all the home languages, including English, to teach greetings, songs, and fingerplays.

- Conduct small groups in the separate home languages. Use the same songs, stories, and discussions in all the language groups.

And here is an at-home suggestion you can try:

- Send families your vocabulary list and describe a topic-related activity they can do with their children. Ask families to review the words and do the activity in their home language.

Honoring Home Languages

It may not be possible to teach the home languages explicitly, as in the previous approach, if you do not have bilingual staff or volunteers available on a regular schedule. However, there are still ways to honor the home languages, in addition to teaching English. For example, in a classroom, the children's families speak Hmong, Somali, Russian, and English. The classroom lead teacher and two assistants are literate in English only. No bilingual educators or volunteers are available to teach in any of the home languages.

English is the primary language of instruction. Most of the classroom materials and books are in English. Some materials and books are in the home languages. Talking, reading, and writing are in English. The class holds two small-group times every day to help the children become more fluent in English. To honor all the home languages, all the children participate in large-group activities that include greetings, songs, and visitors from each language.

Teachers encourage the families to use their home language at home. Families receive ideas and resources related to the classroom curriculum.

Here are some classroom suggestions you can use with this approach:

- Conduct story time in English, with repeated read-alouds to reinforce comprehension.

- Schedule parents or community members to visit on a regular basis to read, sing, or tell stories in the home languages.

- During large-group time, include greetings, songs, and fingerplays in the home languages, adding them to your English repertoire.

- Conduct small groups in English. Use the same stories and discussions in all the groups.

And here is an at-home suggestion you can try:

- Send families your vocabulary list and describe a topic-related activity they can do with their children. Ask families to review the words and do the activity in their home language.

Teaching Infants and Toddlers

The previous suggestions work well for preschoolers. For infants and toddlers, an approach that combines home visits with group experiences works well to support the home languages and introduce English. This approach is used by the Early Head Start program. Families receive a home visit one day per week and attend a classroom session biweekly or monthly. This type of early childhood program is called home visit plus socialization. Such programs give adults and children the chance to socialize with others. The adults get to know other adults and discuss early childhood issues with a teacher. The children get exposure to the classroom, the materials, and the experience of being in a group. For example, in a home visit plus socialization group, the children's families speak Hmong, Spanish, and English. The teacher is literate in English only. All the materials and books are in English.

The teacher talks, reads, and writes in English during the home visit, with help from an interpreter. English is the language of instruction in the socialization classroom, too. To honor all the home languages, all the children are exposed explicitly to greetings, songs, and books from one another's languages.

The teacher encourages families to use their home language at home. Families receive ideas and resources related to the classroom curriculum.

Here are some home-visit suggestions you can try:

- Sing songs and read stories in the home language.

- Encourage the parents to continue to speak the home language.

Here are some classroom suggestions you can try:

- Conduct large-group times in English, repeating the songs and fingerplays so parents and children become familiar with them.

- Add greetings, songs, and fingerplays in the home languages of the families to honor them.

And here is an at-home suggestion:

- Give families your vocabulary list and describe a topic-related activity they can do with their children. Ask families to review the words and do the activity in their home language.

Teaching Home Languages to Children in Kindergarten through Third Grade

In this scenario, an after-school program teaches a home language to children in kindergarten through third grade. The program teaches the home language explicitly for one hour, three to five times per week. Families voluntarily register their children for this program.

The program's curriculum is integrated with the curriculum taught during the rest of the school day. The after-school program uses the same books, or books on the same topic.

Teachers encourage families to use their home language at home. Families receive ideas and resources related to the classroom curriculum.

Reflection Questions

1. Go through your daily schedule and decide what activities you will do to honor the home languages. Implement these activities for two weeks. How is it going? How do you want to proceed?

2. Write a letter to your students' families informing them about your current topic of study and inviting them to collaborate with you. For guidance, use the advice and example on pages 127–28.

Chapter 9

Assessment

Assessment is not just for children. Educators must also assess their environment, their teaching, and their overall program.

The National Association for the Education of Young Children (NAEYC 2009) position statement on assessing dual-language learners states clearly that the aim of assessment should never be to categorize or penalize children. This is particularly important for teachers of dual-language learners to remember, because these children are over-referred to special education. The purpose of assessment is to gain information teachers can use to adapt their instruction so children learn better.

Children cannot learn what we don't teach them. This thought occurred to me after I left a particularly frustrating classroom observation.

The classroom provided high emotional support. The teachers were nice to the children, and the children followed the routines easily. The social-emotional climate was positive.

However, the classroom offered low instructional support. The room was overflowing with clean, age-appropriate materials, but neither the children nor the adults seemed excited as they went about their activities.

The day included circle time with a CD too fast for singing along, cutting and pasting construction-paper ingredients on paper-plate pizzas, and dramatic play in a pizza store by children who did not know the word *apron* or *oven*. The children went from center to center, manipulating objects. The teachers went from center to center, too, acknowledging the children. But the children were not asking questions, and the teachers were not providing intellectual challenges. Everyone was busy, but no one seemed to be learning actively or deeply. No one was curious. They were all just doing, with limited vocabulary and no conversation.

The only active teaching and learning happened during the fifteen-minute reading circle. During this time, the teacher read an interesting book and asked good questions. Four or five children answered the questions, while the rest kept quiet.

When teachers teach young dual-language learners, they need to think about a lot of things. They must consider the children's development and their families' experiences. They have to identify our linguistic and sociocultural goals, and then match their human and material resources to these goals. Then they need to assess all the components of their work: the environment, the teaching behaviors, the families' satisfaction, the overall program, and of course the children's learning. The children's learning should be the goal toward which the other components are aimed. It makes no sense to assess the children's learning without assessing all the other pieces.

In this chapter, I will review some commercially available assessment tools that are scientifically validated and can be used as evaluation instruments in research projects. In addition, I will offer a few tools that I have designed to guide your observations. You may also wish to use tools that you have created yourself, or other instruments that have been useful to you in the past.

Whatever tools you use, I urge you to keep in mind one important concept: Assessing the children's learning is just one of several assessments you must do. Remember that children cannot learn what their teachers don't teach them.

Assessing the Learning Environment

The learning environment is the classroom or family child care home where children learn. The environment includes the space, the materials, and the curriculum. Physical safety is a very important concern, but I will not address that here. My focus is on how the learning environment fosters early literacy and language skills.

The following tools are well designed for assessing the learning environment in relation to early literacy and language skills. They are all published by Brookes Publishing Company (www.brookespublishing .com).

- Early Language and Literacy Classroom Observation for pre-kindergarten (ELLCO Pre-K): This tool will help you assess the presentation and promotion of early literacy skills in a preschool classroom.

- Early Language and Literacy Classroom Observation for elementary (ELLCO K–3): This tool will help you assess the presentation and promotion of early literacy skills in an early elementary classroom.

- Child/Home Early Literacy and Language Observation (CHELLO): This tool will help you assess the presentation and promotion of early literacy skills in a family child care home.

The ELLCO and the CHELLO focus on language and literacy, a critical issue for dual-language learners, but they also address well the classroom climate and the room arrangement. The environment affects how children and teachers feel and how they behave. It is the first place to start. It is the easiest area to fix if the results of the assessment show a need for improvement.

Assessing Instruction

Instruction is not just about teacher style. There are specific skills and behaviors that are more effective than others. Children learn best with good teaching strategies. Dual-language learners need even more careful instruction. Observing a teacher is a challenging task. The observer has to be objective and separate what she feels from what she sees. Therefore it is important to observe classrooms with a critical eye, using a well-designed tool that is reliable (gives consistent results) and valid (accurately assesses what it is constructed to assess). Currently the most comprehensive observation tool for teaching is the Classroom Assessment Scoring System. Its added value is that the rubrics are specific. This makes it a good coaching tool to give feedback to teachers so they can make improvements.

- Classroom Assessment Scoring System (CLASS): This tool assesses the quality of teaching in prekindergarten through third grade based on teacher-student interactions. It is published by Brookes Publishing Company (www.brookespublishing.com).

I designed the following tool to focus instructional observation on behaviors that benefit dual-language learners. It has not been scientifically validated. Its purpose is to guide your observations or self-assessment. This checklist can help you assess your instructional strengths and decide what to do next. In the columns on the right, check the answer that best describes the teaching in your program.

Essential Elements for Teaching

Essential Elements	Always	Sometimes	Never
Educators use home languages whenever possible for comforting children or in urgent or new situations. Educators use positive and caring body language.			
When educators do not know the home language, they use English to comfort children, with special attention to positive and caring body language.			
Educators use English to initiate all their interactions and do not switch languages randomly.			
Educators teach vocabulary in English, scaffolding with gestures, demonstrations, toys, and real objects.			

Essential Elements	Always	Sometimes	Never
When children initiate interactions in English, educators respond in English, even if they know the children's home language.			
When children initiate interactions in the home language, educators who know the language respond in the home language and expand in English.			
Educators supplement large-group reading by reading the same books in English in small groups, using preview-view-review.			
Educators schedule small-group time to give children more opportunities to practice talking.			
Educators actively facilitate play, using scripted dramatic play to promote language learning.			
When children use English, educators respond with encouraging words and actions.			
Educators explicitly acknowledge the different languages spoken in the classroom.			
Educators provide intentional opportunities to talk, read, and write throughout the day.			
When home-language instruction is feasible, it is coordinated with the English curriculum and offered on a predictable schedule. For example, the same book is read and discussed in the home language in a small group.			

Note: A reproducible template of this worksheet is provided in the appendix.

Assessing Family Perceptions and Satisfaction

As you assess your program for dual-language learners, it is important to know what the families think about their experiences with you and what they would like to see happen in the future. You can ask families for feedback in a written survey or orally, with help from an interpreter if necessary. I propose that you ask the open-ended questions provided in the sample family survey that follows. The answers will fall into these general categories:

- curriculum
- learning activities
- schedule
- children's behaviors
- adult behaviors

Once you get all the surveys back, sort the answers into these categories. The sorted feedback will help you decide what to do next. If you want to ask additional questions specific to your program, feel free to add them to the survey.

Family Survey

1. What has your child learned in the past four months? _____

_____

_____

2. Are you happy or unhappy with what your child has learned? Please give an example or two to explain your answer.

_____

_____

3. What would you like your child to learn in our classroom? _____

_____

_____

4. How do you feel about the way your child is learning English? _____

_____

_____

5. How do you feel about the way your child is learning your home language? _____

_____

_____

6. Would you like us to change anything in the way we teach your child? _____

_____

_____

7. Do you plan to change anything in the way you teach your child at home? _____

_____

_____

8. Do you have any other ideas you want to share with us? _____

_____

_____

Note: A reproducible template of this worksheet is provided in the appendix.

Assessing Children's Learning

The NAEYC position statement on assessing dual-language learners, a document titled "Screening and Assessment of Young English-Language Learners," is a thorough and helpful discussion of this topic. I recommend that you read it carefully. It is available at www.naeyc.org/files /naeyc/file/positions/ELL_SupplementLong.pdf.

The scope of this book is too small to comprehensively review learning-assessment tools for dual-language learners. However, I do want to offer you a starting point. Please consider the following tools and continue to research your options.

- **Observing Children Learning English (OCLE):** This tool is available in the appendixes of the book *One Child, Two Languages* by Patton O. Tabors. OCLE is an observation checklist that helps you record and track the progress of children over time.

- **Bilingual Early Language Assessment (BELA):** This is an instrument for bilingual children from 2.9 years to 5 years old. An educator administers it one-on-one in the child's home language and in English. It is available at www.cpsd.us/bela in English, Spanish, Portuguese, Haitian Creole, Arabic, Bangla, and Chinese. It assesses the child's knowledge of basic concepts like body parts, colors, and numbers, as well as the child's linguistic ability in both languages.

- **World-Class Instructional Design and Assessment (WIDA):** This system of assessing English-language learners was developed by researchers at the University of Wisconsin. Its philosophy is that children need to develop strong skills in academic language to succeed in school. For children to progress, the input must match their level of understanding, then become more challenging as children increase their comprehension. The assessment system addresses both social language and academic language. It is available at www.wida.us/assessment.

- **Individual Growth and Development Indicators (IGDIs):** The IGDIs are an efficient tool for monitoring the language and literacy development of three- to five-year-old preschoolers. The IGDIs measure young children's growth over time. The test is developmentally appropriate and easy to administer. It includes three measures: picture naming (assesses expressive language development), rhyming, and alliteration (assesses phonological awareness). You can find free access to the IGDIs at http://ggg .umn.edu/siteindex.html. The IGDIs are available in English only. They are useful for measuring children's English skills.

- **Response to Intervention (RTI):** Response to Intervention is an emerging strategy that is well suited for the teaching and assessment of young dual-language learners. Its philosophy is to assess children and then tailor the instruction to their learning needs. Instruction is delivered in three tiers. In Tier 1, all children in a classroom receive high-quality instruction, as is expected in any excellent classroom. In Tier 2, the children who need more intentional instruction receive it in small groups. In Tier 3, some children get one-on-one instruction, in short segments designed to teach specific skills. The techniques I have described in this book are all examples of best practices for Tier 1 instruction. They can be further modified for smaller groups.

  Here is an example of how Response to Intervention works: Maya and Luis are dual-language learners who speak Spanish at home. They're adapting well to the classroom, but they have small vocabularies. This shows in their tests and in the fact that they don't seem to understand the stories their teacher reads to the class. In addition to the large-group reading in English, Maya and Luis participate in small-group reading in Spanish. And three times per week, each receives a six-minute focused lesson on key vocabulary. During each six-minute lesson, they get to practice individually, and their teacher monitors what they learn.

  In my work as master coach for a statewide early literacy program, I see the benefits of Response to Intervention very clearly. When teachers use RTI, young dual-language learners make fast progress. For more information, visit the website of the National Center on Response to Intervention at www.rti4success.org.

Assessing the Overall Program

In addition to the learning environment, instruction, and children's learning, it is a good idea to assess the program's or school's operations overall. This gives you the big picture. I propose that you use one of the tools described on the next two pages. One is the official tool of Head

Start; the other I have developed. By responding to the items, you will establish whether you have all the elements you need to serve dual-language learners well. The purpose is to make sure that all the systems are in place. For example, either of these tools will inform your decisions on professional development for your educators, and on the materials you need to purchase with your next grant.

- **Program Preparedness Checklist: A Tool to Assist Head Start and Early Head Start Programs to Assess Their Systems and Services for Dual Language Learners and Their Families:** This checklist covers all areas of programming, such as program governance, teacher-child interactions, assessment, and family partnerships. You can find it at http://eclkc.ohs.acf.hhs.gov/hslc/tta-system/cultural-linguistic.

- **Essential Elements for Program Quality:** The checklist on pages 143–44 provides an easy-to-use self-assessment to help you build a high-quality program for dual-language learners. To use the checklist, reflect on the practice of each essential element listed on the left and check on the right whether it happens always, sometimes, or never in your program. (Note: The term *educators* refers to all adults who work with children in the classroom or in a child care home. An educator may be a lead teacher, assistant teacher, bilingual educator, specialist, parent educator, or home visitor.)

Essential Elements for Program Quality

Essential Elements	Always	Sometimes	Never
Classroom staff and administrators understand and can explain the process of second-language learning.			
Classroom staff and administrators understand and can explain the role language plays in academic success.			

Essential Elements	Always	Sometimes	Never
Classrooms are literacy-rich environments as measured by a good observation tool.			
Classrooms have a variety of learning materials (such as toys, books, pictures, and videos) that support the teaching and learning of language.			
The thematic integrated curriculum is rigorous and language rich, with activities tailored for dual-language learners.			
Educators use intentional instructional strategies to teach English.			
Educators use intentional instructional strategies to promote home-language development.			
Children's assessments are developmentally appropriate and measure both cognitive skills and language skills.			
Families receive information on how to support the home language to complement the learning at school.			
Families receive information on how to help their children succeed in the U.S. education system.			
The professional development of all educators and administrators includes cultural and linguistic competence.			
Administrators provide guidance and support to educators through performance evaluation and professional development.			

Note: A reproducible template of this worksheet is provided in the appendix.

Reflection Questions

1. Think about the assessments you are currently using. Are you assessing all components of your work? Which, if any, components are missing? How will you go about choosing the assessments you need to add?

2. Read the sample family survey. What other questions would you like to ask? Write a survey to use in your program.

3. Review the "Essential Elements for Teaching" checklist. Note the items that are already in place in your classroom or in your program. Note the items you want to work on. Choose two to start with. Review your progress in two weeks.

4. Review the "Essential Elements for Program Quality" checklist. Congratulate yourself on the items marked "always." Think about the other items. Which items are you ready to start working on?

Putting It All Together

This book contains a lot of information and advice. How can you put it all together in a way that's useful for you, your students, and their families? Give yourself a little time to ponder your needs and your options, and give yourself some leeway for experimentation. Meanwhile, let's look at Ms. Sheila's classroom for inspiration.

Ms. Sheila's Classroom

Ms. Sheila's preschool classroom served nineteen children. All were four and five years old, and they were headed to kindergarten the following year. Eight children were monolingual English speakers. The other eleven children came from families who spoke Hmong, Spanish, Swahili, French, Somali, and Punjabi at home. Some of the immigrant families were refugees from Laos, Somalia, and Ivory Coast. The others were immigrants from Mexico, El Salvador, and Pakistan. Eight of the dual-language learners were born in the United States.

Such diversity was new for this school. Over the summer, a low-income apartment building opened across the street. Families from all over the world moved in. In late August, the school principal hastily hired a consultant to provide a half-day workshop on teaching dual-language learners. The consultant gave some practical tips for classroom management, suggested useful routines, and shared her belief that preschool programs should help children maintain their home language. She did not address how to teach English to dual-language learners.

At the school's open house, Ms. Sheila noticed that some of her students' families were fluent in English, others were beginners, and a few spoke no English at all. As the families and children conversed, Ms. Sheila observed that some used their home language, others combined English and the home language, and others spoke only in English. What a mix! After the event, Ms. Sheila worried about how she was going to manage this classroom.

Planning for a Multilingual Classroom

First, Ms. Sheila had to plan her staffing. She had one full-time classroom assistant, Ms. Gloria. Like Ms. Sheila, Ms. Gloria was a monolingual English speaker. In addition, the principal allocated the time of three bilingual aides to help Ms. Sheila throughout the week. A Hmong aide would come on Mondays, Wednesdays, and Fridays for thirty minutes each; a Somali aide would come on the same days, also for thirty minutes each, after the Hmong aide left; and a Hispanic aide would come on Tuesdays and Thursdays for one hour each. Ms. Sheila arranged her classroom schedule so the aides would usually visit as center time ended and small-group time began.

Next Ms. Sheila had to think about her classroom's three other home languages (Swahili, French, and Punjabi). How could she develop these home languages with no knowledge of them and no assistance in any of them? Ms. Sheila was also concerned about her English-speaking students. Would their learning be slowed by the pace of their classmates with lower language skills? For example, would Ms. Sheila have to choose simple, predictable books all the time?

Ms. Sheila had to rethink her curriculum, methods, and materials to engage every child and ensure good learning progress. Her pre-K program had high expectations. The children must be ready for kindergarten by spring.

A Typical Day

By the middle of February, Ms. Sheila had worked out solutions to all her major challenges. The following is what happened in her classroom on a typical day.

At 9:00 a.m., parents brought their children to the classroom door. As they entered, Ms. Sheila greeted them with a smile and a friendly comment. For example, "*Bonjour*, Annie. I am happy to see you today. We missed you yesterday!" "Good morning, Leo. I see you are wearing your favorite red shirt today." "*Nyob zoo*, Pao. Your little sister is with you today!" Ms. Sheila started greeting families in their home language at the beginning of the school year. The families loved it right away. This simple act helped her greatly in developing relationships.

After signing in on the white board, where Ms. Gloria was stationed to help children write their names, the children went to the tables and played with small blocks or puzzles. They usually looked at each other's work, smiling and pointing, but they did not talk much. Ms. Sheila didn't urge the children to converse right away in the morning. Instead, she let them make a soft entry into the classroom, reconnecting without pressure.

Twenty minutes into the day, circle time began with a group greeting. Ms. Sheila had a system for this greeting. The greeting was in English on Mondays, Tuesdays, and Thursdays. Wednesdays and Fridays were "United Nations days." On those days, the greeting was in one of the home languages of the dual-language children. The children eagerly anticipated the home-language greetings. The class kept track of the language rotation on a chart. Ms. Sheila reviewed the chart with them every United Nations day. For example, she'd say, "Okay, girls and boys, today is the day for a Spanish greeting. *¡Buenos días, niñas, niños, y maestras! ¡Hoy, vamos a aprender mucho!* [Good morning, girls, boys, and teachers! We are going to learn a lot today!]" As she spoke, Ms. Sheila pointed to the white board, where the words were written. The children then turned to each other, shook hands, and said good morning to their classmates by name. Then they sang a song in the same home language to the tune of "Twinkle, Twinkle, Little Star." By February, the children knew the song well in all the home languages, and they sang in unison.

Circle time proceeded with a limited calendar. Then Ms. Sheila moved on to her main goal for circle time, which was introducing the day's learning activities.

On this day, Ms. Sheila introduced watercolors. She demonstrated how to use the paint box, the small brushes, and the water to paint on the paper. She used simple, accurate language as she showed the children how to paint: "Now I dip the brush into the water jar, and I swirl it around. Then I wipe it lightly on the paper towel, and I decide which color to use. I choose yellow."

Ms. Sheila also presented options for dramatic play and the class project. The dramatic play center included an architecture–interior design studio, a paint shop, and a fabric shop. The class project was remodeling and decorating a large cardboard house. Ms. Sheila introduced the idea that the house needed artwork. She created an artist studio near the house with materials for painting and sculpture.

Ms. Sheila reminded the children about their current topic of study, "colors in my world." This topic was one segment of her thematic integrated curriculum. Throughout the year, she used different themes, for four to six weeks each, to integrate the children's learning of concepts, vocabulary, and skills. She taught the children vocabulary during formal times, such as circle time, reading, and small groups. She encouraged the children to use the words they learned during informal times, such as active learning, meals, transitions, and large-muscle activities. She posted lists of key vocabulary words in strategic places around the room: in the dramatic play area, the block center, and on the lunch tables. These lists helped the adults in the room remember the words and keep their instructional focus.

At the end of circle time, Ms. Gloria read the book *Peter's Chair* by Ezra Jack Keats. She used the repeated read-aloud technique, reading the same book every day for one week. The repetition helped the children learn the vocabulary and plot well. By the end of the week, they could anticipate the story's dramatic moments. They could also retell the story using the words they had learned.

After circle time, the children moved on to active learning for sixty minutes. This hour was an important time for the children to explore and experiment. It was also the time when the bilingual aides came to help.

A Plan for the Bilingual Educators

At the beginning of the year, the aides just hung out. They spent their thirty minutes talking randomly with the children in English or their home language, without a concrete plan. The aides enjoyed playing with the children in their home language, but they felt only marginally useful. Ms. Sheila and Ms. Gloria were grateful to have an extra adult for brief periods, but they felt vaguely frustrated with the aides' role in the classroom. The teachers relied on the aides only to give directions and resolve conflicts: "*Niños, es hora del lunch.* [Children, it's time for lunch.] *Vamos a lavarnos las manos.* [Let's go wash our hands.] *¿Qué te pasa, Ramón? ¿Quieres jugar con el camión azul? Pídeselo a Matthew.* [What's wrong, Ramón? Do you want to play with the blue truck? Ask Matthew if you can have it.] Matthew, Ramón wants to play with the blue truck when you are done with it."

By the end of November, nobody was happy with this haphazard situation. The children were not conversing much. The bilingual aides felt rather lost. Ms. Sheila and Ms. Gloria just used the aides for translation, and because their time was so limited, this service was not very valuable to the class. So the teachers met with the bilingual aides. Together they created a more precise plan that followed the standards of teaching dual-language learners. Their program was not a Head Start program, but they found the Head Start Program Preparedness Checklist very helpful. The chart on the next page shows how Ms. Sheila, Ms. Gloria, and the bilingual educators used the principles and recommendations in the checklist to create a concrete plan for the aides' work in their classroom.

Bilingual Educators in Ms. Sheila's Classroom

Ideas from Head Start Preparedness Checklist	Ms. Sheila's Plan
We promote children's home-language development: Utilize small-group time during the day to introduce or to reinforce concepts in the children's home language.	During small group, the bilingual educators will read the week's book in the home language and discuss it with the children in the home language. This will increase concept development.
We promote children's acquisition of English: We avoid simultaneous interpretation, wherein a staff person speaks to the children in English and then immediately repeats the same information in the home language.	During active learning, the bilingual educators will use their bilingual skills to understand the children's needs and will help the children ask for what they need in their home language or in English, as the situation requires.
We promote positive social and emotional development of preschoolers who are dual-language learners: We pair children who speak languages other than English with English-speaking children for some classroom activities to increase the comfort level of the dual-language learners and help ease their transition.	The bilingual educators will enter the children's play in the home language, if it is a monolingual group. If the children playing together are a multilingual group, the bilingual educators will facilitate conversations in English so all the children interact on a level playing field. When speaking to children in English, the bilingual aides will use gestures, body language, props, and other visual cues to help children's comprehension.
We implement a research-based curriculum that is inclusive of children's languages and cultures: Connect learning to children's prior knowledge and prior experiences. Provide hands-on experiences to make learning interactive and concrete.	Ms. Sheila will inform the bilingual educators of the lesson plans and the current topic of study. The bilingual educators will contribute culturally relevant ideas, pictures, or books.

In addition, Ms. Sheila decided to introduce the bilingual educators formally to all the children. She realized that letting the aides appear and disappear mysteriously throughout the week was confusing for the children. She introduced each aide at circle time: "Boys and girls, I want you to meet Ms. Ana. You have noticed that Ms. Ana speaks Spanish, just as Ema, Jenny, Ramón, and Antonio do at home. Ms. Ana also speaks English. You can speak to her in both languages, Spanish and English. She comes into our room every Tuesday and Thursday. She will read books in Spanish, teach us some Spanish songs, and also play with us in Spanish and English."

With this plan in place, all the adults in Ms. Sheila's classroom felt much better. They knew exactly what to do! And they noticed that all the children—including the English speakers—became more aware of language. For example, five-year-old Matthew said proudly to the Somali bilingual educator one day, "I know a word in Somali: *buug*. That means 'book.'" The classroom truly was becoming a United Nations community of learners.

Making the Most of Every Moment

At the end of active-learning time, the children cleaned up their work and assembled in small groups. Small-group time lasted fifteen minutes. When the bilingual educators were available, the groups were organized by home language. The aides read to the children and discussed the book in their home language. The Somali and Hmong children had home-language small groups three times per week, and the Hispanic children had home-language small groups twice per week.

Ms. Sheila's home-language resources for the children who spoke Punjabi, French, and Swahili were very limited. So she implemented a different plan for these children. The plan had three parts. First, she invited their parents to volunteer in the classroom and read a story, sing a song, or share a dish with the class. This involvement helped their children see that their cultures and languages were interesting and valuable to others. Second, she encouraged the parents to maintain their home language at home, explaining the academic, social, and emotional benefits of doing so. Third, when the bilingual aides held small groups, Ms. Sheila held a small group for the children who spoke Punjabi, French, and Swahili. She read the week's book in English, slowly and with all the props, to give the children extra opportunities to practice listening and talking.

Ms. Sheila's plan was solid. She was both teaching English and supporting home languages. She made good use of her resources. She followed the best practices for teaching dual-language learners. As she continued on her professional journey and served more dual-language learners, she gained more confidence and found more joy in her work.

A Few Last Words

Whenever you teach dual-language learners, you face new challenges and encounter new joys. When you address the challenges, you reap the joys. A successful multilingual classroom can be a vibrant community of people sharing life, language, and learning.

Educators have the chance not only to teach the children but also to support their families. Teachers can encourage families in preserving their home language at home. Educators can also reassure anxious families that their children will learn English at school. Such encouragement and reassurance build warm, constructive relationships.

I have written this book with you, the educator, in mind. I hope it has offered you insights into your own teaching. I hope you find the information and advice useful to your work with dual-language learners and their families. You are shaping the futures of these young people. I wish you the very best in this exciting professional adventure.

Appendix of Reproducible Templates

Brainstorming Worksheet

Classroom Language Plan

Family Story Form

Parent Tips Handout

Essential Elements for Family Support Worksheet

Reading Plan

Essential Elements for Teaching Worksheet

Family Survey

Essential Elements for Program Quality Worksheet

Brainstorming Worksheet

Step 1: Identify and assess staff concerns and engage staff in planning.

_____

_____

_____

_____

Step 2: Clarify beliefs about children as learners.

_____

_____

_____

_____

_____

_____

_____

_____

Step 3: Know the children and their families.

_____

_____

_____

_____

_____

Step 4: Identify your goals for the children.

_____

_____

_____

_____

_____

Step 5: Identify your human resources.

_____

_____

_____

_____

Step 6: Provide training for monolingual English-speaking educators.

_____

_____

_____

_____

_____

Step 7: Provide training for bilingual educators.

_____

_____

_____

_____

Step 8: Identify your material resources.

_____

_____

_____

_____

Step 9: Engage families.

_____

_____

_____

_____

Step 10: Decide how you'll use language in your classroom.

_____

_____

_____

_____

_____

Step 11: Develop a strong thematic curriculum.

_____

_____

_____

_____

_____

Step 12: Brainstorm a plan for teaching dual-language learners and supporting their families.

_____

_____

_____

_____

_____

_____

_____

_____

_____

Classroom
Language Plan

Our Goals for the Children	Sociocultural: Linguistic:
Human Resources	Staff language skills: Family language skills: Volunteer language skills:
Material Resources	

Families' Language Goals	English: Bilingualism: Home language:
Individual Children's Language Skills	English only: Home language only: Bilingual:
Languages in Our Classroom	
Our Thematic Curriculum	

Family Story Form

Hello! We are happy that you are sending your child to our school. We are interested in your well-being, and we want to do a good job of teaching and caring for your child. Please tell us about your family and your child by answering these questions. Thank you.

1. What is your home country? _____

2. How long have you lived in the United States? _____

3. Where did you live before coming to this town? _____

4. What languages did you speak in your home country? _____

5. What languages do you speak in your home now? _____

6. What languages does your child speak at home with you? _____

_____

7. Does your child speak another language with other people? What language? _____

_____

8. What do you want your child to learn from you and your family? _____

_____

_____

_____

9. What do you want your child to learn in our school? _____

_____

_____

_____

10. What parts of your home culture are important to you? _____

_____

_____

_____

11. What parts of U.S. culture are important to you? _____

_____

_____

_____

12. What else would you like us to know about your family and your child? _____

_____

_____

Parents, You Can Help Your Children Be Bilingual!

Keeping up your home language in a new country is not easy. You must work hard at it and not give up. Sometimes children want to speak their home language. Sometimes they do not. It depends on their interest, their personality, and their ability.

You need to have a plan. With planning and effort, you can help your children be bilingual. Your children may not appreciate this gift now, but they will be grateful when they are older. Their thanks will be a nice reward for you.

Here are some tips to keep up your family's home language:

- **Talk with your children all the time.** Talk with your children about everything that happens during the day. You can talk about what to cook for dinner. You can talk about visiting a friend on the weekend. You can talk about a book or magazine article you have read. Speak in your home language even if your children respond in English. If you keep speaking in your home language, your children will continue to understand it.

- **Have a system.** Make a rule about how your family will use your home language and English. This will help your children know what to expect. For example, you might:
  - Speak your home language at home and English at school.
  - Speak your home language at home and English outside your home.
  - Speak your home language with one parent and English with the other parent.

- **Find other people who can speak your home language with your children.** For example, you might:
  - Gather with friends and relatives who live in your community. Go to parties, religious events, or traditional celebrations.
  - Interact with friends and relatives who live in your home country. You can talk to them on the phone. You can also exchange letters and e-mail messages.

- **Watch children's TV shows and videos in your home language. Read books and magazines in your home language.** Some public libraries have children's books and videos in many languages. Ask your local librarian. You can also look for materials at ethnic markets. Organizations of people from your home country may have books, magazines, and videos to share.

- **Visit your home country.** If this is possible, it will immerse your children in your home language. After just a few days in your home country, your children will understand and speak more words in your home language.

- **Set a good example.** If you are bilingual, your children will think it is natural to be bilingual. They will be more interested in both languages.

Essential Elements
for Family Support

Essential Elements	Always	Sometimes	Never
Educators explain to families the process of second-language learning and bilingualism.			
Teachers explain to families the role language plays in academic success.			
Educators teach families how to maintain the home language at home.			
Before a curriculum unit begins, teachers share key vocabulary and concepts with families in English and home languages.			
Educators deliver information about the school and the children in English or home languages as necessary.			
Teachers provide information on how to support children's bilingualism at home.			
Educators share children's assessments with their families.			
Teachers help children and families navigate the U.S. educational system.			
The school is family friendly, with signs and materials in plain English or translated into plain language, culturally competent staff, and interpreters when needed.			

Reading Plan

Book Title:	Date:
Does this book:	**Notes:**
☐ have a predictable text?	
☐ tell a good story?	
☐ convey information?	
☐ have an enjoyable rhythm?	
☐ use repetition?	
☐ challenge or stimulate the children's thinking?	
☐ have an interesting plot?	
☐ have a concrete beginning, middle, and ending?	
☐ depict experiences relevant to the children's daily lives?	
☐ have realistic photographs and illustrations?	

☐ relate to our current topic of study? ☐ take 5–10 minutes to read aloud? ☐ meet the children's comprehension levels? ☐ meet the children's developmental levels?	
Supporting Materials What actions and props can I use to aid the children's comprehension?	
Summary What main ideas (3–6) from the book do I want the children to understand and enjoy?	

Vocabulary What vocabulary words (6–12) do I want to teach from this book?	
Repeated Readings (3–5 per week) When will I read the book? Will I read it to one large group or two half groups?	
Oral Language Skills What are 3 activities related to the story to be done at other times of the day so the children can practice conversation?	

Family Involvement What are 1–3 activities I will use for the school-home link?	
Evaluation How did it go? How did the children react? What did they learn? How did the parents react?	

Essential Elements
for Teaching

Essential Elements	Always	Sometimes	Never
Educators use home languages whenever possible for comforting children or in urgent or new situations. Educators use positive and caring body language.			
When educators do not know the home language, they use English to comfort children, with special attention to positive and caring body language.			
Educators use English to initiate all their interactions and do not switch languages randomly.			
Educators teach vocabulary in English, scaffolding with gestures, demonstrations, toys, and real objects.			
When children initiate interactions in English, educators respond in English, even if they know the children's home language.			
When children initiate interactions in the home language, educators who know the language respond in the home language and expand in English.			
Educators supplement large-group reading by reading the same books in English in small groups, using preview-view-review.			
Educators schedule small-group time to give children more opportunities to practice talking.			

Essential Elements	Always	Sometimes	Never
Educators actively facilitate play, using scripted dramatic play to promote language learning.			
When children use English, educators respond with encouraging words and actions.			
Educators explicitly acknowledge the different languages spoken in the classroom.			
Educators provide intentional opportunities to talk, read, and write throughout the day.			
When home-language instruction is feasible, it is coordinated with the English curriculum and offered on a predictable schedule. For example, the same book is read and discussed in the home language in a small group.			

Family Survey

1. What has your child learned in the past four months? _____

_____

_____

2. Are you happy or unhappy with what your child has learned? Please give an example or two to explain your answer.

_____

_____

_____

3. What would you like your child to learn in our classroom? _____

_____

_____

4. How do you feel about the way your child is learning English? _____

_____

_____

5. How do you feel about the way your child is learning your home language? _____

_____

_____

6. Would you like us to change anything in the way we teach your child? _____

_____

_____

7. Do you plan to change anything in the way you teach your child at home? _____

_____

_____

8. Do you have any other ideas you want to share with us? _____

_____

_____

Essential Elements for Program Quality

Essential Elements	Always	Sometimes	Never
Classroom staff and administrators understand and can explain the process of second-language learning.			
Classroom staff and administrators understand and can explain the role language plays in academic success.			
Classrooms are literacy-rich environments as measured by a good observation tool.			
Classrooms have a variety of learning materials (such as toys, books, pictures, and videos) that support the teaching and learning of language.			
The thematic integrated curriculum is rigorous and language rich, with activities tailored for dual-language learners.			
Educators use intentional instructional strategies to teach English.			
Educators use intentional instructional strategies to promote home-language development.			
Children's assessments are developmentally appropriate and measure both cognitive skills and language skills.			

Essential Elements	Always	Sometimes	Never
Families receive information on how to support the home language to complement the learning at school.			
Families receive information on how to help their children succeed in the U.S. education system.			
The professional development of all educators and administrators includes cultural and linguistic competence.			
Administrators provide guidance and support to educators through performance evaluation and professional development.			

Glossary

academic language: The language of learning. Academic language involves words not heard in daily conversations. It is the language of comparing, classifying, inferring, synthesizing, and analyzing. An example of academic language use by a four-year-old is describing the sequence of events in the book *Little Red Riding Hood* or explaining how a caterpillar becomes a butterfly. Academic language is sometimes called cognitive academic language proficiency (CALP).

acculturation: The modification of an individual as a result of contact with a different culture.

additive bilingualism: The idea that a second language can be added to the first language without the loss of the first language.

BICS: Basic interpersonal communication skills, or social language.

bilingual/bilingualism: The ability to speak two languages. Sometimes the terms *biliterate* and *bilingual* are used interchangeably.

bilingual educators: Paraprofessional staff members in a school or program who assist the teacher in the classroom. They can also serve as interpreters and translators for families. Sometimes they are called cultural navigators.

biliterate: Having the ability to listen, talk, read, and write proficiently in two languages.

CALP: Cognitive academic language proficiency, or academic language.

code switching: Changing from one language (code) to another within one sentence or conversation. Code switching is sometimes called language mixing.

cultural guide: A person who has a respectful way of giving information about a culture to a person of another culture. A cultural guide listens to what someone already knows about a culture and provides additional information tailored to that person.

culture: The beliefs, customs, history, language, and art of a group of people. Culture shapes people's daily experiences, memories, and understanding of life.

developmentally appropriate practice: A method for teaching young children (birth to eight years old) that takes into consideration the developmental stage of the child. It combines teacher-led activities with child-initiated activities. The activities are neither too difficult nor too easy. For example, it is developmentally appropriate to ask a beginning dual-language learner a yes-or-no question. It is not developmentally appropriate to ask the same child an open-ended question. Developmentally appropriate practice is sometimes called DAP. DAP is fundamental to the philosophy of the National Association for the Education of Young Children.

dominant culture: The culture most people accept as the standard for everyday behaviors such as language and manners.

dual-language learner: A child who is learning two languages. Babies, toddlers, preschoolers, and early-elementary-age children are at the beginning of learning their first language. Their second language may be introduced at birth or during these early years. Therefore, they are learning two languages at the same time.

explicit instruction: Instruction that clearly tells the student what he is going to learn, demonstrates the information, and allows the student to practice so he can learn the skill.

expressive language: The language we speak. Expressive language develops after receptive language, and it develops in stages.

formulaic speech: Copying expressions children have heard others use successfully, such as *hey*, *pretty good*, *bye-bye*, and *stop*. Sometimes second-language learners at the formulaic speech stage use repetition for emphasis, with rhythm that sounds like a complete sentence.

higher-order thinking: The ability to infer, make predictions, and think about cause and effect.

intentional teaching: Teaching with a concrete plan for what the children should be learning.

interpreter: Person who provides oral translation.

language development and communication: How children learn to listen, speak, read, and write.

linguistic goal: A goal that outlines the language or languages the program wants the children to learn. For example, the goal may be for the children to learn English in the classroom. In that case, specific teaching strategies have to be put in place to ensure this happens.

metalinguistic awareness: The ability to think about how language works, not taking it for granted. For example, young bilinguals learn early that every object has two words.

monolingual: A person who knows one language.

multilingual: A person who knows multiple languages.

phonological awareness: The ability to discriminate sounds in spoken language. Two important skills for learning to read are alliteration (beginning sounds in words) and rhyming (ending sounds in words).

productive language: A form of expressive language that marks the final stage of language learning. Children are using productive language when they know enough words and useful phrases to build their own sentences.

proficient bilingualism: The ability to talk, read, and write in two languages. A proficient bilingual is someone who has equally strong knowledge of both languages.

projects: A curriculum approach in which children study a particular topic in depth. The teacher chooses the topic or gathers ideas by observing children's interests. Once the class establishes a general topic to study, they ask, "What do we want to find out?" The teacher and children develop vocabulary and activities together, starting with what the children know and adding new words, concepts, and investigations as they ask questions about the topic.

readability level: The difficulty of a document can be measured to determine the approximate grade level in reading.

receptive language: The language we understand. Receptive language develops first in the process of learning a language.

semilingualism: Knowing two languages without being proficient in either. For example, having the ability to make social conversation, but not to read and write in both languages.

silent period: A phase of language learning when children keep quiet and take the time to listen and process what they hear. They also watch for cues in body language, the environment, the actions of other children, and pictures in books.

social language: The language of home and community used for everyday life events, activities, and relationships. An example of social language for a four-year-old is talking about what happened during a visit to grandma's house. Social language is sometimes called conversational language or basic interpersonal communication skills (BICS).

sociocultural goal: A goal that outlines a positive approach for helping children learn about their own culture and the culture of others. For example, the goal may be for English-speaking children to learn about the culture of their friends from other cultures and for dual-language children to learn about American culture.

subtractive bilingualism: The idea that for a person to develop fully, a second language must replace his first language.

target words: The words that are most important to know in order to understand a story or text.

telegraphic speech: Showing objects and pointing, using isolated words such as *juice* or *truck*, and using two-word combinations such as *me play*, *car go*, and *play house*.

thematic curriculum: A curriculum approach similar to projects but more teacher directed. The teacher chooses a topic relevant to the children's lives, researches the information, provides all the materials, and proposes all the activities.

translator: Person who provides written translation.

Recommended Resources

Center for Applied Linguistics (CAL)
www.cal.org

The Center for Applied Linguistics provides a comprehensive range of research-based information, tools, and resources related to language and culture. CAL is a private, nonprofit organization in Washington, D.C. It focuses on bilingualism, English as a second language, literacy, foreign-language education, dialect studies, language policy, refugee orientation, and the education of linguistically and culturally diverse adults and children.

Colorín Colorado
www.colorincolorado.org

Colorín Colorado is a bilingual website (in English and Spanish) for families and educators of English-language learners. It is an educational initiative of public television station WETA of Washington, D.C., in collaboration with the American Federation of Teachers, the National Institute for Literacy, and the U.S. Department of Education. Its free web-based service provides research information, activities, and practical advice for educators and Spanish-speaking families of English-language learners.

Culture for Kids
www.cultureforkids.com

Culture for Kids is a seller of books, DVDs, games, and other educational materials from every part of the world for children and parents. For example, one intriguing item is *The Parent's Homework Dictionary*, which explains American concepts for homework assignments in nine different languages.

Early Childhood Learning and Knowledge Center
http://eclkc.ohs.acf.hhs.gov

This website is a service of the Office of Head Start. It offers information and tips for parents, teachers, and administrators on all aspects of early childhood. The Office of Head Start includes the National Center for Cultural and Linguistic Responsiveness, and the website includes a section dedicated to dual-language learners and their families. The "Program Preparedness Checklist" is available here. This checklist helps programs assess whether their systems, policies, and procedures meet the needs of children and families who speak languages other than English. It provides useful information for program planning and professional development.

FPG Child Development Institute
www.fpg.unc.edu

The FPG Child Development Institute, formerly called the Franklin Graham Porter Center, is part of the University of North Carolina at Chapel Hill. It is a multidisciplinary organization that studies young children and their families. More than two hundred researchers, students, and staff work on projects dealing with parent and family support; early care and education; child health and development; early identification and intervention; equity, access, and inclusion; and early childhood policy. In addition, FPG publishes curricula, resource guides, reports, and articles.

Mantralingua

www.mantralingua.com

Mantralingua is an online bookstore that sells children's books and games in fifty-two languages. Its goals are to provide resources for minority languages around the world and to celebrate the cultural and linguistic nature of society.

Milet

www.milet.com

Milet is a multilingual publisher that has titles in twenty-six languages. Milet publishes an extensive collection of dictionaries on CD, as well as other materials for children and adults.

Multilingual Books

www.multilingualbooks.com

Multilingual Books is an online bookstore offering children's books in one hundred languages. Most are bilingual with English. Well-known favorites, such as *Brown Bear, Brown Bear, What Do You See?* and *Goldilocks and the Three Bears*, are available in languages such as Urdu, Tamil, and Arabic. The website also offers DVDs, CDs, and software for children and adults.

National Association for Bilingual Education (NABE)

www.nabe.org

NABE represents both bilingual learners and bilingual education professionals. Its five thousand members include educators, researchers, policy makers, and parents in twenty states. Its mission is to advocate for bilingual learners and their families and to promote native-language as well as English proficiency. The association works toward intercultural understanding and respect.

National Association for the Education of Young Children (NAEYC)

www.naeyc.org

NAEYC is a member organization with three hundred local, state, and regional affiliates. Its mission is to improve the well-being of all children from birth to eight years old by improving the quality of early childhood programs, teachers, and caregivers through adherence to developmentally appropriate practice. The organization sponsors and produces professional development conferences and educational materials, including position statements on major issues such as the teaching and assessment of dual-language learners.

National Center for Cultural Competence
http://nccc.georgetown.edu

The National Center for Cultural Competence is located in the Center for Child and Human Development at Georgetown University. It provides training, technical assistance, and consultation; contributes to knowledge through publications and research; creates tools and resources to support health and mental health care providers and systems; and supports leaders to promote and sustain cultural and linguistic competency.

National Center for Learning Disabilities
www.ncld.org

The National Center for Learning Disabilities provides information and promotes research on effective learning. It addresses the needs of dual-language learners.

National Clearinghouse for English Language Acquisition and Language Instruction Educational Programs (NCELA)
www.ncela.gwu.edu

NCELA supports the U.S. Department of Education's Office of English Language Acquisition, Language Enhancement, and Academic Achievement for Limited English Proficient Students (OELA). It provides information on research, funding, and legislation. It is operated by the George Washington University Graduate School of Education and Human Development.

Plain Language
www.plainlanguage.gov

This website was created by the Plain Language Action and Information Network (PLAIN), a group of federal employees who support the use of clear communication in government writing. They develop and maintain the content of this site. It contains information on the Plain Writing Act of 2010, and many resources to keep writing clear and free of jargon.

United Nations Country Profiles

www.un.org/esa/population/publications/countryprofile/profile.htm

The United Nations Country Profiles provide information about the languages, people, geography, history, economy, and politics of countries around the world.

U.S. Citizenship and Immigration Services (USCIS)

www.uscis.gov

USCIS is the government agency that oversees lawful immigration to the United States. Its website provides a wealth of information to help you understand issues that immigrant families may be dealing with.

U.S. Department of State Background Notes

www.state.gov/r/pa/ei/bgn

The U.S. Department of State background notes provide up-to-date information on the languages, people, geography, history, economy, and politics of countries around the world.

WIDA: World-Class Instructional Design and Assessment

www.wida.us

This website introduces visitors to a system of thinking about English-language learners developed at the University of Wisconsin. WIDA's philosophy is that children need to develop strong skills in academic language to succeed in school. For children to progress, the input has to match their level of understanding, then progress as children increase their comprehension. The assessment system addresses both social language and academic language.

References

August, Diane, and Timothy Shanahan, eds. 2006. *Developing Literacy in Second-Language Learners: Report of the National Literacy Panel on Language-Minority Children and Youth.* Mahwah, NJ: Lawrence Erlbaum.

Barrera, Isaura, and Robert M. Corso. 2003. *Skilled Dialogue: Strategies for Responding to Cultural Diversity in Early Childhood.* Baltimore: Brookes.

Bialystok, Ellen. 2001. *Bilingualism in Development: Language, Literacy, and Cognition.* New York: Cambridge University Press.

Bialystok, Ellen, and Kenji Hakuta. 1994. *In Other Words: The Science and Psychology of Second-Language Acquisition.* New York: Basic Books.

Boss, Pauline. 1999. *Ambiguous Loss: Learning to Live with Unresolved Grief.* Cambridge, MA: Harvard University Press.

Bunce, Betty H., and Ruth V. Watkins. 1995. *Language Intervention in a Preschool Classroom: Implementing a Language Focused Curriculum.* Baltimore: Brookes.

Burns, M. Susan, Peg Griffin, and Catherine E. Snow, eds. 1999. *Starting Out Right: A Guide to Promoting Children's Reading Success.* Washington, DC: National Academy Press.

Castro, Dina C., Betsy Ayankoya, and Christina Kasprzak. 2011. *The New Voices Nuevas Voces Facilitator's Guide to Cultural and Linguistic Diversity in Early Childhood*. Baltimore: Brookes.

Cho, Eun Kyeong, Dora W. Chen, and Sunghee Shin. 2010. "Supporting Transnational Families." *Young Children* 65 (4): 30–37.

Collins, Molly Fuller. 2005. "ESL Preschoolers' English Vocabulary Acquisition from Storybook Reading." *Reading Research Quarterly* 40 (4): 406–8.

Copple, Carol, and Sue Bredekamp. 2009. *Developmentally Appropriate Practice in Early Childhood Programs Serving Children from Birth through Age 8*. Washington, DC: National Association for the Education of Young Children.

Cummins, Jim. 2000. *Language, Power, and Pedagogy: Bilingual Children in the Crossfire*. Clevedon, UK: Multilingual Matters.

———. 2001. "The Academic and Political Discourse of Minority Language Education: Claims and Counter-Claims about Reading, Academic Language, Pedagogy, and Assessment as They Relate to Bilingual Children's Educational Development." Summary of paper presented at the International Conference on Bilingualism, Bristol, April 20, 2001. http://iteachilearn.org/cummins/claims.html.

Curtis, Deb, and Margie Carter. 2003. *Designs for Living and Learning: Transforming Early Childhood Environments*. St. Paul, MN: Redleaf Press.

Dalai Lama and Howard C. Cutler. 2009. *The Art of Happiness in a Troubled World*. New York: Doubleday.

DeBruin-Parecki, Andrea, and C. Timion. 1999. *Building Intercultural Friendships through Story Development and Socialization: A Middle School/University Partnership*. Orlando: National Reading Conference.

Dickinson, David K., and Patton O. Tabors. 2001. *Beginning Literacy with Language: Young Children Learning at Home and School*. Baltimore: Brookes.

Espinosa, Linda M. 2010. *Getting It RIGHT for Young Children from Diverse Backgrounds: Applying Research to Improve Practice*. Special ed. Washington, DC: National Association for the Education of Young Children.

Fortuny, Karina, Randy Capps, Margaret Simms, and Ajay Chaudry. 2009. *Children of Immigrants: National and State Statistics*. Washington, DC: Urban Institute.

Fortuny, Karina, Donald J. Hernandez, and Ajay Chaudry. 2010. *Young Children of Immigrants: The Leading Edge of America's Future*. Children of Immigrants Research, August. Washington, DC: The Urban Institute.

Freeman, David E., and Yvonne S. Freeman. 2001. *Between Worlds: Access to Second Language Acquisition*. 2nd ed. Portsmouth, NH: Heinemann.

Genesee, Fred. 2007. "A Short Guide to Raising Children Bilingually." *Multilingual Living Magazine* January/February, 24–31.

Genishi, Celia, and Anne Haas Dyson. 2009. *Children, Language, and Literacy: Diverse Learners in Diverse Times*. New York: Teachers College Press.

Gillanders, Cristina. 2007. "An English-Speaking Prekindergarten Teacher for Young Latino Children: Implications of the Teacher-Child Relationship on Second Language Learning." *Early Childhood Education Journal* 35 (1): 47–54.

Gonzalez-Mena, Janet. 2008. *Diversity in Early Care and Education: Honoring Differences*. Boston: McGraw-Hill.

Greenman, Jim. 2005. *Caring Spaces, Caring Places: Children's Environments That Work*. Redmond, WA: Exchange Press.

Gunnar, Megan R., Erin Kryzer, Mark J. Van Ryzin, and Deborah A. Phillips. 2010. "The Rise in Cortisol in Family Daycare: Associations with Aspects of Care Quality, Child Behavior, and Child Sex." *Child Development* 81 (3): 851–69.

Halliday, M. 1978. *Language as a Semiotic*. Baltimore: University Park Press.

Harper, Candace, and Ester de Jong. 2004. "Misconceptions about Teaching English-Language Learners." *Journal of Adolescent and Adult Literacy* 48 (2): 152–62.

Hart, Betty, and Todd Risley. 1995. *Meaningful Differences in the Everyday Experience of Young American Children*. Baltimore: Brookes.

Hatch, Evelyn. 1992. *Discourse and Language Education*. New York: Cambridge University Press.

Helm, Judy Harris, and Lilian G. Katz. 2011. *Young Investigators: The Project Approach in the Early Years*. 2nd ed. New York: Teachers College Press.

Hernandez, Donald J., Nancy A. Denton, and Suzanne E. Macartney. 2008. "Children in Immigrant Families: Looking to America's Future." *Social Policy Report* 22 (3): 3–12.

Herrell, Adrienne L. 2000. *Fifty Strategies for Teaching English Language Learners*. Upper Saddle River, NJ: Merrill.

Hill, Jane D., and Kathleen M. Flynn. 2006. *Classroom Instruction That Works with English Language Learners*. Alexandria, VA: Association for Supervision and Curriculum Development.

Jameson, Judith. 1998. "Three Principles for Success: English Language Learners in Mainstream Content Classes." *From Theory to Practice* 6. Tampa, FL: Center for Applied Linguistics.

Kauerz, Kristie. 2010. *PreK–3rd: Putting Full-Day Kindergarten in the Middle*. Policy to Action Brief, no. 4. New York: Foundation for Child Development.

Keyser, Janis. 2006. *From Parents to Partners: Building a Family-Centered Early Childhood Program*. St. Paul, MN: Redleaf Press.

Kim, Karl H. S., Norman R. Relkin, Kyoung-Min Lee, and Joy Hirsch. 1997. "Distinct Cortical Areas Associated with Native and Second Languages." *Nature* 388: 171–74.

Kotulak, Ronald. 1997. *Inside the Brain: Revolutionary Discoveries on How the Mind Works*. Kansas City, MO: Andrews McMeel.

Krashen, Stephen D. 1981. *Second Language Acquisition and Second Language Learning*. New York: Pergamon Press.

Krashen, Stephen D., and Tracy Terrell. 1983. *The Natural Approach: Language Acquisition in the Classroom*. New York: Pergamon Press.

Laosa, Luis M., and Pat Ainsworth. 2007. "Is Public Pre-K Preparing Hispanic Children to Succeed in School?" *Preschool Policy Brief* 13. New Brunswick, NJ: National Institute for Early Education Research.

Lesaux, Nonie K., and Linda A. Siegel. 2003. "The Development of Reading in Children Who Speak English as a Second Language (ESL)." *Developmental Psychology* 39 (6): 1005–19.

Liu, Yi-Juin, Alba A. Ortiz, Cheryl Y. Wilkinson, Phyllis Robertson, and Millicent I. Kushner. 2008. "From Early Childhood Special Education to Special Education Resource Rooms: Identification, Assessment, and Eligibility Determinations for English Language Learners with Reading-Related Disabilities." *Assessment for Effective Intervention* 33 (3): 177–87.

Lynch, Eleanor W., and Marci J. Hanson, eds. 2004. *Developing Cross-Cultural Competence: A Guide for Working with Children and Their Families*. 3rd ed. Baltimore: Brookes.

Martínez, Rubén. 2004. *The New Americans*. New York: New Press.

Mather, Mark, and Patricia Foxen. 2010. *America's Future: Latino Child Well-Being in Numbers and Trends*. Washington, DC: National Council of La Raza.

Mead, Sara. 2011. *PreK–3rd: Principals as Crucial Instructional Leaders*. Policy to Action Brief, no. 7. New York: Foundation for Child Development.

Minnesota Department of Education and Minnesota Department of Human Services. 2005. *Early Childhood Indicators of Progress: Minnesota's Early Learning Standards*. Roseville: Minnesota Department of Education.

Minnesota Literacy Council. 2012. "National Literacy Facts." Accessed May 17. http://mlc.themlc.urbanplanet.com/National_Literacy_Facts.html.

Montanaro, Silvana. 2001. "Language Acquisition." *North American Montessori Teachers Association (NAMTA) Journal* 26 (2): 1–7.

NAEYC (National Association for the Education of Young Children). 2009. *Where We Stand on Assessing Young English Language Learners*. Position statement. Washington, DC: NAEYC.

National Center for Education Statistics. 2011. Average Reading Scale Scores of 4th- and 8th-graders in Public Schools and Percentage Scoring at or above Selected Reading Achievement Levels, by English Language Learner (ELL) Status and State: http://nces.ed.gov/programs/digest/d11/tables/dt11_134.asp.

Nemeth, Karen N. 2009. *Many Languages, One Classroom: Teaching Dual and English Language Learners*. Beltsville, MD: Gryphon House.

Office of Head Start. 2010. "Program Preparedness Checklist: A Tool to Assist Head Start and Early Head Start Programs to Assess Their Systems and Services for Dual Language Learners and Their Families." Early Childhood Learning and Knowledge Center. http://eclkc.ohs.acf.hhs.gov/hslc/tta-system/cultural-linguistic/docs/program-preparedness-checklist-v-5.pdf.

Ogbu, John. 1991. "Immigrant and Involuntary Minorities in Comparative Perspectives." In *Minority Status and Schooling: A Comparative Study of Immigrant and Involuntary Minorities*, edited by Margaret A. Gibson and John Ogbu, 3–33. New York: Garland.

Passe, Angèle Sancho. 1994. "A Model for Training Family Educators in Multiculturalism." Master's thesis, University of Minnesota.

———. 2010. *Is Everybody Ready for Kindergarten? A Tool Kit for Preparing Children and Families*. Saint Paul, MN: Redleaf Press.

Pearson Zurer, Barbara. 2008. *Raising a Bilingual Child: A Step-by-Step Guide for Parents*. New York: Living Language.

Pianta, Robert C., Karen M. LaParo, and Bridget K. Hamre. 2008. *Classroom Assessment Scoring System Manual Pre-K*. Baltimore: Brookes.

Planty, Michael, William Hussar, Thomas Snyder, Grace Kena, Angelina Kewal Ramani, Jana Kemp, Kevin Bianco, and Rachel Dinkes. 2009. *The Condition of Education 2009*. Washington, DC: National Center for Education Statistics, Institute of Education Sciences, Department of Education. http://nces.ed.gov/pubs2009/2009081.pdf.

Russakoff, Dale. 2011. "PreK–3rd: Raising the Educational Performance of English Language Learners (ELLs)." Policy to Action Brief, no. 6. New York: Foundation for Child Development.

Schickedanz, Judith A. 2008. *Increasing the Power of Instruction: Integration of Language, Literacy, and Math across the Preschool Day*. Washington, DC: National Association for the Education of Young Children.

Slavin, Robert E., and Alan Cheung. 2005. "A Synthesis of Research on Language of Reading Instruction for English Language Learners." *Review of Educational Research* 75 (2): 247–84.

Smith, Miriam W., Joanne P. Brady, and Louisa Anastasopoulos. 2008. *Early Language & Literacy Classroom Observation Pre-K Tool (ELLCO Pre-K)*. Baltimore: Brookes.

Snow, Catherine E. 2004. "English Language Learners: Boosting Academic Achievement." *Research Points* 2 (1).

Snow, Catherine E., M. Susan Burns, and Peg Griffin, eds. 1998. *Preventing Reading Difficulties in Young Children*. Washington, DC: National Academy Press.

Tabors, Patton O. 2008. *One Child, Two Languages: A Guide for Early Childhood Educators of Children Learning English as a Second Language*. Baltimore: Brookes.

Thomas, Wayne P., and Virginia P. Collier. 1998. "Two Languages Are Better Than One." *Educational Leadership* 55 (4): 23–26.

U.S. Department of Education. 2008. *Biennial Report to Congress on the Implementation of the Title III State Formula Grant Program*. Washington, DC: U.S. Department of Education.

Villegas, Ana María, and Tamara Lucas. 2002. *Educating Culturally Responsive Teachers: A Coherent Approach*. Albany: State University of New York Press.

Vukelich, Carol, James Christie, and Billie Enz. 2002. *Helping Young Children Learn Language and Literacy.* Boston: Allyn and Bacon.

Wasserman, Leslie Haley. 2007. "The Correlation between Brain Development, Language Acquisition, and Cognition." *Early Childhood Education Journal* 34 (6): 415–18.

Young, Russell. 1991. *A Paradigm for Examining Multicultural Education.* Paper presented at the annual meeting of the American Educational Research Association, Chicago, April.

Index